Manifold
DESTINY

VILLARD BOOKS • NEW YORK • 1989

Manifold DESTINY

THE ONE! THE ONLY! GUIDE TO COOKING ON YOUR CAR ENGINE

Chris Maynard and Bill Scheller

Copyright © 1989 by Chris Maynard and Bill Scheller
Illustrations copyright © 1989 by Robert Paul Scudellari

Library of Congress Cataloging-in-Publication Data

Maynard, Chris
    Manifold destiny: the one! the only! guide to cooking on your
car engine/by Chris Maynard and Bill Scheller.
        p.   cm.
    ISBN 0-679-72337-4
    1. Cookery.   2. Automobiles—Motors.   I. Scheller, Bill.
II. Title.
TX652.M335   1989
641.5′8—dc20   89-40194

All interior photographs by Chris Maynard
Illustrations by Robert Paul Scudellari
Designed by Oksana Kushnir

Manufactured in the United States of America
9 8 7 6 5 4 3 2
First Edition

For Pluggy and Molly

Contents

Manifold
DESTINY

In Which We Get Started, and Ask the Question "Why Bother?"

Neither of us can leave Montreal without stopping first at Schwartz's, on Boulevard St.-Laurent.

Schwartz's is a little storefront deli that cures and smokes its own beef briskets, which it heaps high in the front window partly for display and partly so the countermen can quickly spear and slice them. "Smoked meat" is what Montreal prosaically calls this apotheosis of pastrami, and Schwartz's makes the best. You can eat it in the store. You can take it out and eat it at home. Or you may have to eat it on the sidewalk half a block away when the aroma coming through the butcher paper drives you nuts. What we had in mind, one summer's day in 1985, was to pack some in the car for a rest-stop picnic on our way back to Boston.

We were barely out of the city when we started to talk about what a shame it was that our pound of Schwartz's wouldn't be so alluringly hot when we pulled over for lunch. When you order this stuff the way Montreal insiders do—"easy on the lean"—room temperature just doesn't do it justice.

It was then that the idea hit. One of us remembered those stories we used to hear thirty years ago, about lonely truckers cooking hot dogs and beans on their engines. Why not Schwartz's smoked meat? It wouldn't even be cooking it—Schwartz had already done that—but just borrowing a little heat from the engine to warm it up. So we decided what the hell; if it worked for Teamsters, why not us?

We pulled off the interstate in Burlington, Vermont, bought a roll of aluminum foil, and triple-wrapped the sliced brisket. Opening the hood, we spied a nice little spot under the air filter of the '84 VW Rabbit, which seemed the perfect place to tuck in the package, and off we went. An hour later we arrived at a standard-issue Vermont highway rest stop, the kind that looks like they wash the trees, and *voilà!*—in minutes, we were putting away hot smoked-meat sandwiches that actually had steam rising off them. Best of all, we nearly made two women at the next picnic table choke on their sprouts when they saw that instead of a busted fan belt, we had actually just dragged our lunch from the Rabbit's greasy maw.

Necessity, to rewrite the old chestnut, is the mother of necessary inventions—like ways to heat smoked meat when you don't have a steam table handy. But since inspired foolishness is the *real* hallmark of civilization, it wasn't long before we were inventing necessities. For instance, a dire need to roast a pork tenderloin on I-95 between Philadelphia and Providence. Car engines, we discovered, are good for a lot more than simply heating things up.

Soon we were calling each other (not on car phones, thank God) with news of our latest accomplishments:

"I poached a fillet of sole."

"I roasted a stuffed eggplant."

"I figured out how to do game hens."

"I made baked apples."

Before long, those rest-stop stares of disbelief had been replaced by reactions infinitely more delightful to savor—like that of the toll collector who swore he smelled chicken and tarragon, but couldn't figure out where the hell it was coming from.

What we didn't realize, during those early years of random experimentation, was that our burgeoning skills as car-engine cooks were going to serve us splendidly as we competed in one of the most grueling sporting events on the planet: the Cannonball One Lap of America Rally. The One Lap is an eight-thousand-mile-plus highway marathon, seven days of nonstop driving in which participants must adhere to strict rules while reeking of spilled coffee and unchanged underwear. It might be the most exhausting and disorienting event anyone would pay money to enter, but of course it makes you feel like a kid with nothing to do except ride his bike in the park for a week—with no grown-ups around.

Trouble is, it's damned difficult to stick to the rally routes and get anything decent to eat. Most people who run the One Lap follow a regimen of truck-stop breakfasts (not necessarily eaten at breakfast time) and assorted pack-along calories drawn from the canned and bottled food groups. Our wonderful epiphany, shared by none of the fifty-seven other teams in the 1988 event, was that if we cooked on the big V-8 under the hood of our sponsor's stretch Lincoln Town Car, we could eat like epicures without screwing up our time and distance factors.

Here's what we did. Two days before the rally started in Detroit, we worked out a menu and did our shopping. Then we commandeered the kitchen of our friend Marty Kohn, a feature writer for the *Detroit Free Press,* and put together enough uncooked entrées to last us at least all the way to our midway layover in Los Angeles. Boneless chicken breasts with prosciutto and provolone, fillet of flounder, a whole pork tenderloin, a ham steak (a reversion to our simple heat-through days) —everything was seasoned, stuffed, and splashed according to our own recipes, sealed up tightly in three layers of aluminum foil, and promptly frozen. We felt like we were turning Marty's kitchen into a tiny suburban version of those factories where they make airplane food, with one big difference—our stuff was good.

The next day we transferred our frosty little aluminum packages to the kitchen freezer at the Westin Hotel in the Renaissance Center (try pulling a request like *that* on the next concierge you meet) and had them brought up with our coffee and croissants on the morning of the rally. The food went into a cooler, the cooler went into our Lincoln, and off we went. Every afternoon between Detroit and the West Coast we'd haul out another dinner, throw it on the engine, and cook it as we lopped a few hundred more miles off the route. Let our competitors use the drive-thrus at McDonald's. We ate well, very well indeed.

We would have done the same thing in L.A. for the return trip, but we didn't have the time. Anyway, it occurred to us somewhere around Albuquerque that we *couldn't* have done it, since none of the people we know in L.A. have freezers. Everyone there eats out all the time, subsisting entirely on a diet of langoustine ravioli on a coulis of roasted red peppers.

By the time the rally ended, we'd gained more fame for our means of sustenance than for our position in the final standings: Everybody, it seemed, had something to say about car-engine cooking. Half the comments were expressions of pure disbelief (and this book is an attempt to convert the disbelievers), while the rest amounted to variations on "Truck drivers have been doing that for years." *Please.* All the truck drivers we've ever heard of who cook on their diesels are still punching vent holes in cans of Dinty Moore stew.

This is not to say we refuse to acknowledge the pioneers. We are by no means the first people to cook food on car engines. The idea dates back so far, in fact, that it predates cars altogether.

The Huns of the fourth and fifth centuries lived on horseback, and subsisted to a great extent on meat. When a Hun wanted to enjoy a hunk of unsmoked brisket—say, when he was tearing around in the One Lap of the Western Roman Empire (with points for pillage) —he would take the meat and put it under his saddle cloth, and the friction between Hun and horse would have a tenderizing and warming effect. (We think they used saddle cloths. If not, well, just don't think about it.) Since this was a situation in which a "cooking" effect was achieved by the application of excess heat generated by the means of propulsion, it is clearly part of the line of descent that leads to hot lunch buckets in the cab of a steam locomotive, and to stuffed chicken breasts à la Lincoln Town Car. We can't say for sure, but it may also have been the origin of steak tartare.

But let's get back to that important qualification— *excess heat generated by the means of propulsion.* This dis-

qualifies a lot of other attempts at mobile cookery, or at least relegates them to a different branch of evolution. We read recently, for instance, that the big, handsomely outfitted carriage Napoleon Bonaparte used during his military campaigns was equipped with an oil lantern mounted above and behind the rear seat that could be used for cooking as well as lighting. But whether or not the little corporal used his lantern to heat up leftover veal Marengo, the fact is that lanterns don't make carriages go. What Napoleon was really on to here was the ancestor of the latest yuppie doodad, the dashboard microwave. Don't laugh—these are hard upon us, touted as just the thing for people too important to waste time revving up the molecules of frozen Danish in their kitchens. The traffic accident of the future will involve some boob who, peeling a memo off his on-board fax machine, doesn't see the lady in the next lane taking a Pop-Tart out of her micro.

No such risk with car-engine cooking. Since you can't check to see if your dinner is done without getting out of the vehicle and looking under the hood, it's no more dangerous than pulling over to change a tire—a lot less dangerous, in fact, since you don't get to pick the location for a flat tire. As engine cooking spreads in popularity—which it will—interstate rest areas will take on a new, homey character. People will ask each other what smells so good, and lend each other oven mitts; those two rich farts in the Grey Poupon ad who are always borrowing each other's mustard will be joined by plenty of ordinary folks. Like most slow, low-tech enterprises, car-engine cooking will bring people together. Don't take this lightly; the only other way to promote sociability on the road is to smile at strangers in the Howard Johnson's, and God knows where that could get you.

But ultimately, gastronomy overrides sociability. The best reason to cook on your car engine is the same desire to avoid indigestion that motivated us during the rally. Unless you're carrying with you the collected works of Calvin Trillin or Jane and Michael Stern and have the time to detour to all the wonderful diners and rib joints they have chronicled, a long car trip is likely to bring you up short in the eats department. And it's not like the good old days were any better. We recently came across Henry Miller's *The Air-Conditioned Nightmare*, based on a six-month cross-country trip he took in a '32 Buick back in 1941. Miller finished the trip in Los Angeles, not only dyspeptic over the philistines and materialists he claimed to have encountered all over the republic, but with his innards devastated from eating in one greasy spoon after another. Poor devil—that '32 Buick probably had a lovely flathead six, as choice a cooking device as any six-burner restaurant range. If only he'd known. And being Henry Miller, he'd probably have felt better about America if only he'd known that in little more than a decade the philistines and materialists at Rambler were going to produce a car with a backseat that folded into a bed.

But we digress. The point is that you can make better meals for yourself, on your engine, than the vast majority of the roadside stands can make for you. Not to mention that engine cooking is a great way to sample regional foods. Think about crayfish in Louisiana. Lake perch in Wisconsin. Abalone in Northern California (look ahead, if you must, to our abalone recipe). And think of the fun you could have on vacation, with endless, monotonous rides made bearable by salivating over that dinner cooking right under your own hood. Instead of "When are we going to get there?" the kids will ask, "When will the chicken be done?" Finally, the car-engine chef is using one of the tastiest and most healthful cooking methods, simmering foods in their own juices in a sealed package—*en papillote,* as they say when they cook on their Renaults in France.

We could go on, maybe even mentioning the conservation benefits of cooking with heat that otherwise would be wasted—at the risk, of course, of sounding like refugees from the 1970s gas shortage Moral Equivalent of War. But who knows? If there's another energy crisis, we might be hailed as the heralds of a kinder, gentler way to cook dinner.

2

Beginner's
Luck—and Skills

Half an hour in traffic proves that any dolt can drive, but your first experiences in the kitchen no doubt convinced you that it takes at least a marginally able dolt to make dinner.

While we'll assume that you pass muster on that score, there are nevertheless a trunkful of tips and techniques peculiar to car-engine cooking that you must understand before you start dribbling chicken fat down the side of your exhaust manifold. To paraphrase David Byrne—This ain't no Hotpoint, this ain't no micro, this ain't no fooling around. . . .

HERE'S YOUR ENGINE

Like everything else, car engines used to be a lot simpler. There was a straightforward, uncluttered engine block, with a valve cover either on top or off to one side. A carburetor and intake manifold got the fuel/air mixture into the engine, and an exhaust manifold branched to each of the cylinders to carry off the hot, spent gases of combustion. All the other components—distributor, starter, fuel pump, radiator, fan, and so forth—stood out plain and simple. In fact, the single most plentiful thing under your old hood was air. If you were working on your engine in those days, and dropped a wrench, it fell through and landed on the ground.

Today, the ground is one thing you *won't* see when you look under the hood. What with power assists for braking and steering, air-conditioning, fuel injection, turbocharging, emission controls, and the electronic paraphernalia that drives you batty with dashboard commands to shift gears at absurdly low RPMs, today's engine compartment looks like an unkempt spare-parts drawer at NASA. As far as things like fuel savings and pollution abatement go, this is all to the good. (If the greenhouse effect gets much worse, you can forget car-engine cooking and just fry eggs on the sidewalk.) But the cluttering of engine compartments with gadgetry has posed a challenge for the cook.

It's frustrating as hell now to find the perfect spot for a package of chicken thighs, only to find it's already taken by the vacuum-assisted pressure sensor for the snibulator pump. We remember reading a story in one car magazine in which a guy described his father's early-fifties technique of securing cans of baked beans to his manifold with baling wire. Aside from the fact that the whole purpose of this book is to take you beyond beans, we defy anyone to find two spots on a modern car engine from which a length of baling wire could be safely secured. For that matter, we defy you to find baling wire, unless your kitchen-on-wheels was manufactured by John Deere.

Still, there is a positive side to this tangle of technology. Inadvertently, it often affords small crannies in which food packages can be wedged tightly (which ties in with the current "portions for one" trend) as well as miles of wiring and tubing that can be used to hold food in place.

But let's throw it into reverse for a second. Despite all these changes—and the fact that many engines are now mounted sideways so they can link up with the transaxle for front-wheel drive—the basic automotive power plant still shares certain elemental design features with its clean-lined forebears. Engines, for instance, are still defined by the number of cylinders they have: in the vast majority of cases, eight, six, or four. The exceptions are the mighty twelve-cylinder Jaguars (roast beef, with plenty of room left over for Yorkshire pudding) and BMWs, and three-banger Third World-mobiles like the Chevy Sprint. (You can *probably* cook on the motors of this class of vehicles, but only if you find the recipe manual for one of those kiddie ovens that bakes brownies with a light bulb.) Anyway, all of these machines burn fuel—hence the term *internal combustion* —and in the process, all of them get hot.

Ah, but how hot is hot, and what parts get hottest? The first thing we should point out is that we're not talking about "engine temperature" as it is expressed by the idiot light or, if you're lucky, the gauge on your dashboard. Strictly speaking, the dash indicator isn't giving you the temperature of the engine but of the coolant circulating between the radiator and the block. If you have a real gauge, the number in the middle, where the needle is supposed to be, is most likely 220;

the number up at the end—highlighted in a frantic shade of red—is probably 260. This latter figure is intimately associated with the phenomenon of sweaty guys with their cars pulled over to the side of the Garden State Parkway in August, hoods up and rubbery-smelling steam pouring out into the pure Jersey summer air. You don't ever want to hit 260.

No, we're not talking coolant temperature. What we're interested in is the actual temperature of the exposed metal parts of the engine, surfaces that can be a hell of a lot hotter than the coolant circulating beneath them. We've heard the figure 600 degrees Fahrenheit bandied about (and are willing to believe it as far as the exhaust manifold is concerned), but for our purposes we don't care as much about numbers as results. If you want to play Mr. Wizard, you could buy a couple of those high-temperature thermometers that people stick on their wood stoves and stovepipes (to tell them when to adjust the dampers) and affix them to different surfaces of your engine. We never bother with this, because (a) it is too troublesome and scientific (our dampers are maladjusted too), and (b) on a modern engine, surfaces are so broken up that your foil-wrapped food is likely to be in contact with several components at once. What we favor is the time-trusted method of temperature verification known as "burn your finger." This is simple. Just get your engine up to operating temperature, turn off the ignition, lift the hood, and touch metallic things with your finger until you burn it. Not third-degree, just the kind of quick hit where you pull your hand back fast and stick your finger in your mouth. Forget trying this on any parts made of plastic—there's a lot of it under the hood nowadays—because it will never get hot enough to do anything more than mildly warm things.

Remember, you aren't necessarily looking for the hottest spots. Car-engine cooking is an extremely inexact science, and there is plenty of opportunity to balance fast cooking on a very hot surface vs. slow cooking on a not-so-hot surface.

Successful engine cooking comes down to these two questions: How far are you driving? and When do you expect to be hungry?

Besides, cooking temperature is just one consideration. You're looking for not only a place that's hot enough, but one that's commodious and secure enough. We'd much rather take an hour longer to cook a package of stuffed eggplant in a large enough cranny that wasn't roaring hot than to jam it into the seventh circle of hell and run the risk of having the foil break or, worse yet, the whole package fall out onto the road. (You try to retrieve an eggplant in traffic, and we're not responsible.)

An inexact science, to be sure. We'd love to be able to tell you what location will cook each dish the best on each and every car engine, but the vast number of differences in engines and related components and in the cooking requirements of various foods makes this impossible. What we can do is offer the accompanying diagrams on basic engine configuration and throw in a few tips on different engine parts—and different cars —that we've had experience with. Read up, then roll up your sleeves and resort to the empirical method.

You've probably noticed that we talk a lot about exhaust manifolds. As we said before, this is the hottest part of the engine surface because it carries the gases that are the waste products of combustion in the cylinders. From here, they go through the muffler to the exhaust pipe, then into the atmosphere to threaten civ-

IT'S NOT MOM'S KITCHEN, BUT....

Some car fanciers seem to be awestruck by the sight of a big V-8 nesting in a sea of tubes and hoses. From a culinary point of view, cooking on one of these is like trying to do a seating arrangement in the Collier brothers' apartment. Just remember, all those doodads are there for a reason. Whether it's good or bad, don't move them if they don't want to go.

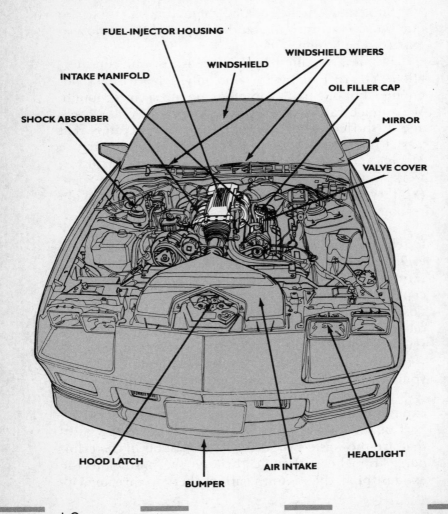

FUEL-INJECTOR HOUSING

WINDSHIELD WIPERS

WINDSHIELD

INTAKE MANIFOLD

OIL FILLER CAP

SHOCK ABSORBER

MIRROR

VALVE COVER

HOOD LATCH

AIR INTAKE

HEADLIGHT

BUMPER

HOT AS IN HOTPOINT

Turbocharging, as on this Chrysler Corporation four-cylinder model, is a popular method of squeaking enough power out of a small engine to satisfy both the EPA and those bozos who think streaks of black rubber point to their manliness. To us, it's just one more oven obstacle.

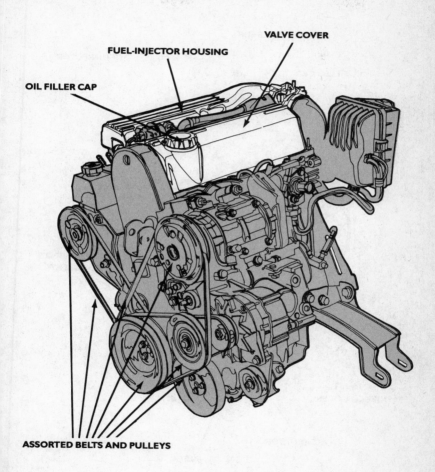

VALVE COVER

FUEL-INJECTOR HOUSING

OIL FILLER CAP

ASSORTED BELTS AND PULLEYS

SMALL ENOUGH FOR A STUDIO

Here's a neat little apartment-size model four-cylinder engine. The fluted
valve cover on top will put nice sear lines on your steaks; with a little ingenuity
you should be able to fix a couple of fish fillets on the slanted exhaust manifold guard.

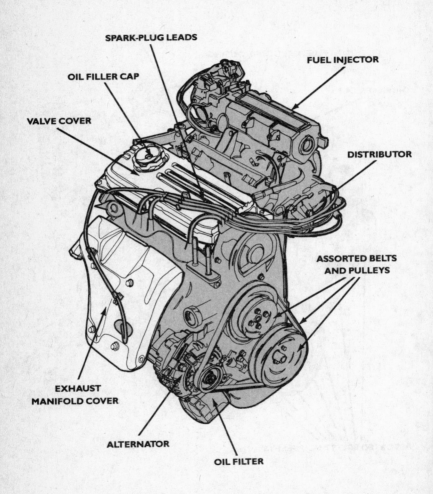

SPARK-PLUG LEADS

FUEL INJECTOR

OIL FILLER CAP

VALVE COVER

DISTRIBUTOR

ASSORTED BELTS
AND PULLEYS

EXHAUST
MANIFOLD COVER

ALTERNATOR

OIL FILTER

ilization. If you have an old car with a fully exposed and easily accessible exhaust manifold (see diagram), you've got a nice, quick cooking surface—provided you have a way to keep food secured to the engine. Modern engines, on which any number of external contraptions obscure much of the manifold, actually often compensate for increased cooking time by providing more nooks and crannies for tucking. If you can't take advantage of direct heat from the manifold, don't despair; just take a longer ride and figure that you're cooking in an oven instead of on a barbecue grill.

Actually, you don't need the exhaust manifold at all. On an old V-8, you should have plenty of space for less intense cooking on top of the engine block itself, alongside the carburetor and beneath the air filter.

NOTE: When exploring the possibilities of this territory, *never* put anything where it will interfere with the free movement of the accelerator linkage. Also, *never* think you can use the air-filter housing as a warming oven, no matter how much empty space there seems to be in there.

Even smaller cars have their engine-top possibilities —remember, that historic first package of Schwartz's smoked meat was wedged alongside the air filter of a four-cylinder diesel Rabbit.

The best setup we have ever come across for easy-access, top-of-the-engine cooking was the upper surface of the in-line six in a 1965 Jaguar XK-E. If you can think of no other reason to own an E-type Jag—in which case your soul is as dead as a road-kill armadillo —consider that long, uncluttered block, the top of

Five No-nos

1. Interfering with free movement of the accelerator linkage. This is a spring-loaded device that connects the gas pedal with the carburetor or fuel-injection system, thus regulating the flow of fuel to the cylinders. If it jams, either you won't go or you won't stop. *Give it a wide berth.*

2. Blocking the flow of air into the engine's air intake. Internal combustion requires gas and air. *Let your motor breathe.*

3. Indiscriminate yanking on wires, hoses, and so forth to secure food packages. Better you eat at a burger joint than pull out a spark-plug wire. *If the package doesn't fit, don't force it.*

4. Placing, checking, or removing food with the motor running. Being a fan belt means never having to say you're sorry. *Come back with the same number of fingers you started with.*

5. Foil-wrapping foods with too much liquid. Aluminum foil may make a wonderful customized cooking vessel, but a pot it's not. No car owner's manual calls for basting the engine.

which is formed into a deep *V* by the slanted valve covers on either side. The plugs come in right at the top, but they hardly interfere. This is the place for roasting elongated items like pork tenderloin or eye of the round. What's more, the cooking area is so nicely exposed that you never even have to get grease on your bony, aristocratic knuckles where they poke through the holes on your driving gloves. Until Subaru comes out with an optional tepinyaki grill, the Jag gets our convenience award.

Spark plugs can actually be as much of a help as a hindrance. When you find them set into a recess deep enough to require an extension on your socket wrench at tune-up time, you've also found a good spot to insert small, individual items like boned chicken thighs. If the plug recesses are close to the exhaust manifold on one side of the engine, the food placed there will cook faster, so, depending on the recipe, stop along the way and move your packages from one side to the other. Otherwise, you could be embarrassed—as we once were—by baked apples baked only halfway across. (We haven't baked apples since, but feel free to give them a try.)

Fuel injection, now standard on most makes, presents some interesting possibilities. Look under the hood of a new car and you'll see a shiny flat surface, usually made of cast aluminum and about nine or ten inches square, that sits right up top on the middle of the engine. That's the housing for the fuel-injection apparatus. While there are often little niches beneath which you can jam things between the housing and the engine block, what we're really interested in is that griddlelike expanse up top. We first tried it in the Lincoln Town Car we drove in the One Lap of America rally, and were disappointed to find that it was only good for warming precooked things like cured ham steak with a side of baked beans. That shouldn't have surprised us, since the fuel injectors aren't a source of heat, and the housing top is pretty far removed from the fiery innards of the engine. But we reasoned that since a good deal of ambient heat is trapped under the hood, and the housing *is* made of a conductive material, it was worth another try. (After all, Calphalon pots are made of aluminum, aren't they?)

Our faith in the injector housing was vindicated on a drive up the Maine coast in an '88 Chrysler New Yorker. Atop that flat aluminum surface we placed two foil packages, each containing a stuffed and partially boned Rock Cornish game hen. After two hours of driving we opened one package and discovered that the hens were not only cooking, they were browning beautifully. We flipped the packages over, got back on the road, and ate the little hens, done to a turn, after only four hours of touring the scenic Maine coast.

When you start cooking on fuel-injector housings, there's an important caveat: You have to come to grips with the critical issue of hood clearance. If there's too much clearance, your food is going to fall off. And if there isn't enough, you're going to slam down the hood and squash the packages, break the foil, and make what can only be described as a big mess. (The game hens, by the way, flattened just enough, rather like a pressed galantine; this probably helped them cook as well as they did.)

So here's the strategy. Before you put any food on the injector housing, make a cone of aluminum foil about four or five inches high. Put it on the housing and shut the hood. Now lift the hood and see how much the cone has been flattened. Too much? You'll have to cook flat food, like fish fillets. Not very? Then wad some additional foil and place it atop your packages of food to hold them in place. It's that simple.

Once in a while, you'll come across a particular model whose designer seems to have been thinking about your needs as a car-engine cook. We once rented

AN OLD PRO TURNS ON HIS STOVE

An experienced engine chef lovingly places dinner atop the fuel-injector housing on a Pontiac V-6. He's already done the foil-cone test (see page 24) and knows the hood will keep it secure. He also knows enough to keep his bare fingers away from the hot metal.

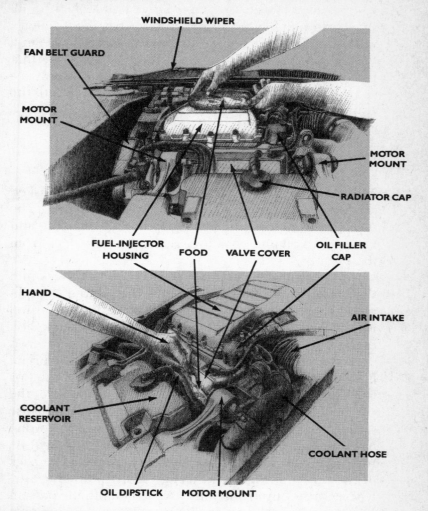

WINDSHIELD WIPER

FAN BELT GUARD

MOTOR MOUNT

MOTOR MOUNT

RADIATOR CAP

FUEL-INJECTOR HOUSING   FOOD   VALVE COVER   OIL FILLER CAP

HAND

AIR INTAKE

COOLANT RESERVOIR

COOLANT HOSE

OIL DIPSTICK   MOTOR MOUNT

A SMALL PORTION FOR A SMALL DIET

If you've got a small appetite (we don't) and can make do with small portions, there are some bite-size places on the engine available for cooking. Here, our chef wedges an appetizer between the valve cover and the oil dipstick. Wedgies like this are best removed slowly and carefully.

an '88 Toyota Camry; we immediately popped the hood to size up the kitchen and discovered, next to the right wheel well, a big square empty space that looked for all the world like a bun warmer. As to what the Toyotans were thinking about when they put a bun warmer in a Camry, we have no idea. Since theirs is a culture that places no great stock in baked goods, we can only assume that this was yet another canny ploy to play to the American market.

WILL IT SMELL FUNNY?

This is not a particularly bright question, but it is asked so often that we may as well finally lay it to rest. The usual phrasing is "Won't the food end up smelling and tasting like oil and gas?" or "Is there any danger from the exhaust?"

Let's put the answer this way. When you check into the Hotel Cipriani in Venice and throw your complimentary terry-cloth bathrobe over the heated towel rack, do you worry about getting it wet? Of course not, because you know the hot water that heats the towels is *inside* the pipes that make up the rack. If it isn't, Cipriani is in big trouble—the same as you are if there's oil or gas sloshing around under your hood outside the proper channels. (If the leak is bad enough to cause serious food contamination, your engine probably won't be running long enough to cook anything anyway.) As for exhaust, it should come out of the pipe at the back of the car. If it is leaking through faulty plumbing anywhere farther up front, it is likely to get into the passenger compartment and enable you to discuss your next meal with Escoffier himself.

Still, the outer surfaces of a car engine are seldom squeaky-clean, and by "blackened" Paul Prudhomme doesn't mean tainted with crud from a valve cover— aside from what bogus Cajun menus in suburban fern bars may lead you to believe. This is why one of the first rules of car-engine cooking is this: Wrap everything

A Cook's Comparison of Ten Late-Model Car Engines

A systematic appraisal of the cooking capabilities of every automotive-engine configuration ever manufactured would be the car chef's equivalent of the *Larousse Gastronomique,* and would doubtless fill as many pages. Such a comprehensive appraisal is obviously outside the scope of this book, but in order to get you thinking about what to look for, we have stuck our heads under the hoods of ten representative 1989 models. A list such as this cannot outline all of the possibilities each engine presents; resourceful road cooks will likely find toasty spots that have slipped, both literally and figuratively, between the cracks in this chart.

And don't forget older models. The title of this book, after all, is derived from the exhaust manifold, and it is on vintage iron that this tubular griddle, lately interred beneath mounds of Flash Gordon plumbing, will most likely show itself. But don't feel bad if you're stuck with a brand-new car. Cooking on and around injector housings (successors to the intake manifolds of yore) and valve covers is a subtle and rewarding art.

See following pages

27

MAKE AND MODEL	ENGINE DESIGNATION	FUEL-INJECTOR-HOUSING COOKING SURFACE
Chevrolet Celebrity GL	V-6 2.8 Liter FI*	9" x 11"[1]
Chrysler New Yorker/ Dodge Dynasty	V-6 3.0 Liter FI	8" x 12"[3]
Corvette[7]	V-8 5.7 Liter FI	12" x 5½" (use front ⅔ only)[8]
Jeep Cherokee	In-Line 6 4.0 Liter FI	N/A[11]
Lincoln Town Car[14]	V-8 5.0 Liter FI	11" x 13"
Mercedes-Benz 560 SEL[15]	V-8 5.6 Liter FI	inaccessible
Pontiac Grand Prix	V-6 2.8 Liter FI	8–10" x 11"[17]
Porsche 928S	V-8 5.0 Liter 32 valve FI	3" x 13" (two parallel surfaces)[20, 21]
Toyota Camry	V-6 2.5 Liter 24 valve FI	4½" x 5"[23]
Toyota 4x2 Minitruck	V-6 3.0 Liter FI	10" x 13"[25]

* FI = Fuel Injection
[1] A nice flat surface; looks like a cross-section of a Parma ham.
[2] Good for flat pieces, such as sole fillets.
[3] The Cornish-game-hen cooker par excellence.
[4] Hardly necessary on these models—the fuel-injector housing, both above and beneath, is more than enough.
[5] Ample space between valve cover and fuel-injection ports.
[6] Plus a few side dishes.
[7] Entire top of engine looks like an anodized anteater.
[8] Port structure (four pairs of tubes) good for Vienna sausage and other hors d'oeuvres.
[9] Too close to road; also a real arm-burner if you try to reach it.
[10] It's a two-passenger automobile.
[11] Exhaust manifold and fuel-injection apparatus covered by a flat metal stamping, roughly 6" x 16" with several small obstructions. Plenty of cooking room, and highly accessible.
[12] See #11.
[13] Irrelevant to cooking. See #11; sheet-metal area is to right of valve cover as you face car.

EXHAUST-MANIFOLD COOKING SURFACE	FOIL-CONE TEST (HOOD-TO-INJECTOR-HOUSING CLEARANCE)	VALVE COVERS	SERVINGS
3" x 12"[2]	1½"	inaccessible	6
inaccessible[4]	1⅝"	14" x 4"[5]	4[6]
inaccessible[9]	1¼"	12" x 4" (left) 8" x 4" (right)	4[10]
[12]	N/A	[13]	4
inaccessible	2¾"	15" x 4"	4
inaccessible	N/A	inaccessible	[16]
inaccessible	1⅞"	13" x 3"[18]	3 large or 4 small[19]
inaccessible	1¾"	9" x 3" (right); (left inaccessible)[22]	3
7½" x 2" (slight curve)	1¾"	14" x 6"	3[24]
partially accessible[26]	2¼"	3¼" x 6"	6

[14] Entire engine is at incipient boiling point visually.

[15] Entire business area of engine is covered by a flat piece of steel, square at the back and curved at the forward end; it looks like the cover to Hermann Göring's toilet seat.

[16] Let them eat cake.

[17] An irregular trapezoid; doesn't get very hot.

[18] Exposed in front, and it gets pretty hot. But it's hard to figure how you'd keep stuff from falling off.

[19] Better for warming than cooking, unless you can solve problem posed in #18.

[20] If you wrap a veal steak tightly and press it down, you'll get nice sear marks in block letters saying PORSCHE 32V.

[21] The eight injector tubes fold beautifully into a valley, overlapping like the hills along Highway 101 near Santa Barbara. Good for nestling soft stuff like pureed squash.

[22] Good assortment of lugs for securing packages.

[23] Good spots in and among port tubes beneath housing; great for sausages.

[24] Bun warmer behind left front wheel.

[25] Nice fluting for an interesting impression on your steak.

[26] Perhaps space for a couple of chicken thighs.

three times in aluminum foil. It makes checking for doneness a bit of a pain, but it virtually guarantees a hermetic seal that locks flavor in and dirt out. Remember, *three times*. No more, no less.

FOOD SELECTION AND PRECOOKING PREP WORK

Although the Triple Foil Wrap rule is the key to successful car-engine cookery, there are a few other dos and don'ts that, when applied with a dose of the plentiful highway commodity called common sense, will assure that things get done properly (or, in cooking terms, properly done).

First off, keep your recipes simple. You'll notice that along with regional variety, simplicity was one of the main criteria in our selection of recipes. This is not because we believe, like the Shakers, that it's a gift to be simple; on the contrary, much of what is really fun and worth doing in this world is, like nature itself, idiotically complex. Gilt lilies are the very stuff of life: We once boned a whole capon, stuffed it with alternating layers of chicken mousseline, duxelles, and spinach soufflé, and wrapped it in brioche. But we had the good sense to cook it in an oven, not on a car engine.

One thing to remember is to avoid recipes that involve a lot of liquid, since this will make the foil packages easier to puncture, and messier if they do. (The only exceptions to this rule are situations involving cans or semirigid containers, and engines—such as classic, unadorned flatheads, or the power plant on a Greyhound bus—that can accommodate them.) Also, you're better off if the foods you wrap can be contoured against hot parts of the engine, preferably with the bulky foil seam on the outside, for better contact and heat distribution. (See sidebar.) Don't use cuts of meat, fish, or poultry that are too thick. And bones, if left in, will make packages too rigid—as well as increase cooking time.

There isn't much to be said about food placement that wasn't already covered when we talked about engine configuration. When they designed your car engine, they also designed its available cooking surfaces, and what you see is what you get. Keep in mind, though, that you can compensate for lack of direct heat by increasing cooking time, or for excessive heat by decreasing cooking time. We found that boned chicken thighs, for example, cook just as nicely on the exhaust manifold of an Olds Cutlass as on the fuel-injector housing of a Dodge 600. The only difference is that you have to drive the Dodge twice as far.

When you do decide on a surface to use, watch out for sharp protuberances that might puncture your foil wrapping. Little nubs and knurls can be handy, though.

Wrapping Techniques and Aluminum-Foil Brand Comparisons

We've all wrapped our share of leftovers.

Bundling up meals for engine cooking is a similar procedure, only more precise—like wrapping Christmas presents. First, make sure nothing you're wrapping is going to poke through the foil (chicken-wing tips can do this). If you spot potential trouble, wrap the pointy parts loosely, wadding foil as necessary to provide a cushion on the innermost foil layer; the two subsequent layers can be wrapped more snugly. Second, leave enough foil on the sides to make a secure, overlapping fold. (Use extra-wide foil if necessary.) Bring the foil up around the top of the food and make a flat, interlocking seam, like the ones on a pair of good blue jeans, and tuck the excess underneath on both sides. You might try alternating the direction of the seams (top to bottom) on each successive wrapping, but if all your seams run on top of each other, be sure to put the seamless side of your package against the engine for better heat distribution.

You'll notice that we haven't recommended heavy-duty foil. Try it if you want; we find it behaves no better than the standard variety. As for whether to put the shiny or matte-finish side out, we feel it makes no difference. The shiny surface does make for a better display, though, when you're showing off to your friends.

Last but not least, be careful when unwrapping, since you may want to rewrap to continue cooking. All aluminum foils become brittle when heated, as heat rearranges the molecules in their crystalline structures into a more orderly pattern.

Here are the results of tests we have had performed on four popular brands of aluminum foil. The purchases were made in Providence, Rhode Island, in February 1989.

BRAND NAME[1]	THICKNESS[2]	PRICE PER 75 SQ. FT.[3]	GOOD HOUSEKEEPING SEAL	STRUCTURAL INTEGRITY	SHINY SURFACE	KOSHER?[4]
Sun Glory	.0004 in.	$1.39	No	None	Mirror-like	Ⓚ
Stop & Shop	.00045	1.49	No	Acceptable (that .00005 makes a difference)	Slight brushing	Ⓚ
Star	.0006	1.62	No	Pretty good	Pronounced parallel brushing running lengthwise	Ⓤ
Reynolds	.0006	1.79	Yes	Best; stays unwrinkled	Same as Star	Ⓤ

[1] All packages have double-edged cutting bar staked to the box. This appears to be an industry standard.
[2] All thickness figures represent an average of multiple measurements.
[3] Prices may vary.
[4] We have no idea of the religious attributes of aluminum foil.

Chris Maynard and Bill Scheller

ALL WRAPPED UP
What can we say about wrapping with tinfoil? We can say: Do it neatly, do it tightly, do it thrice.

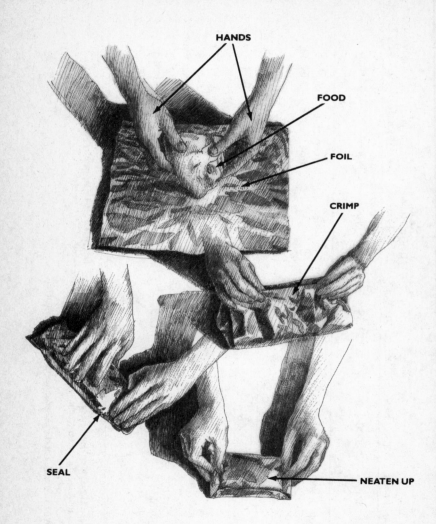

HANDS

FOOD

FOIL

CRIMP

SEAL

NEATEN UP

Find That Rolls!

Consider the phantom 1920s Rolls-Royce, a car we heard about from a curbside well-wisher in Manitou Springs, Colorado, when we stopped for lunch during the big rally. This guy was watching us conduct a fuel-injector-housing foil cone test (while at lunch, plan for dinner), and told us that he had heard of a Jazz Age Rolls that had had a little oven cast right into the engine block. A special touring model, he said it was. Did this wonderful car ever exist? And if it did, was it one of a kind, or an extremely limited production model? Why wouldn't the PR people at Rolls talk with us when we called them? Why, if what they were trying to come up with was a Toyota-style bun warmer, didn't they call this edition a "Buns-Royce"? Why would they do that, when "Buns-Royce" sounds like a dancer at Chippendale's? Why is there being rather than nothingness?

Ask questions, son, it's the only way you'll learn anything.

(opposite page)

Step 1—Place food in center of sheet of foil.

Step 2—Pulling foil snugly against your lunch, crimp tightly to make a good seal.

Step 3—Fold ends toward center of package and crimp again.

Step 4—Neaten up by pressing foil into a snug package with no protruding flaps to catch and tear during cooking.

Repeat two more times so food is securely wrapped in three layers of foil.

We've had some success with wrapping packages so that excess foil at the ends can be used as tabs to twist around protruding parts, thus holding the food in place. Use what you can find: the oil dipstick, the narrow tubing associated with the emissions-control system, you name it. Just don't run your tabs across too wide a gap—aluminum foil ain't baling wire.

So much for the mechanical angle. The remainder of what there is to be learned about car-engine cuisine has to do with how food behaves, and with the different modes of cooking and the foods to which they are best suited.

Forget boiling. At first you might think that a car engine is a great place to boil things, because there's no way you can watch the pot. But think about it: Even if you found a hot enough spot on the motor, and a cooking vessel that would fit it, you'd have about as much success boiling something in there as Chrysler did putting a record player in the glove compartment of '57 DeSotos. (Don't laugh; they tried it.) You'd leave a trail of soup, even on the smoothest roads.

Likewise, don't think you can roast anything to a crispy stage of doneness—the best you can hope for is a nice browning, as we got with the game hens on the injector housing of the Chrysler New Yorker. This you try to accomplish by minimizing the liquid in your recipe, or keeping it on the engine long enough and in a hot enough spot for the liquid to cook away and leave the surfaces to brown.

What you *can* do nicely is braise foods—cook them gently in a small amount of liquid, just enough to transfer the heat and serve as a vehicle for seasonings. This is where wine comes in handy, as in our recipe for

Poached Fish Pontiac (page 103)—but remember to keep that opened bottle in the trunk. When you're working with something delicate, like fish fillets or veal, also be sure to rub the inside of your innermost sheet of foil with plenty of butter or oil to prevent sticking.

Then there's a whole class of apparently simple low-rent dishes that at first glance seem made for car-engine cooking, but which we emphatically do not recommend. We hadn't really thought about grilled cheese, for instance, until we ran across a piece in *The New York Times* about an unnamed "famous and rich performer" who, while traveling the world and staying in swank hotels, always carries a roll of aluminum foil and a clothes iron. Upon arriving in a city before a performance, she heads for the nearest food store and picks up some cheese and a loaf of bread. She makes cheese sandwiches, wraps them in the foil, and cooks them under the iron in her hotel room.

This goofy maneuver presents a certain dilemma. On the one hand, it's pretty tacky and takes advantage of a free energy source (the hotel's electricity), and on those counts we're in favor of it. But there are two drawbacks. First, the bread and cheese you're likely to pick up at five-thirty on a Sunday afternoon in Moscow, Idaho, probably won't be the kind you'd really want to eat. It would be a lot simpler to just get something like a Stewart System Styrofoam-and-cheese concoction and let some sleazy bartender heat it in the micro. After all, your travel iron probably doesn't serve drafts.

The second drawback is that room service, especially in the best hotels (we're assuming that you're not always traveling through places like Moscow, Idaho), is one of the crowning glories of Western civilization. If you can pick up the phone, press one button, and cause food and drink to magically appear at your door, why bother burning your fingers heating bad cheese and white bread into an indistinguishable colorless mass under an iron that you have to lug all over the place?

Or on your car engine. One of the points in favor of engine cooking is that it allows you to enjoy good food that you've made yourself using good ingredients. If you're just going to start heating and melting, you're only slumming, like Miss Famous-and-Rich.

At the other end of the spectrum, there are the fad cooking techniques. The Westin Hotel in Calgary, Al-

berta, for instance, has lately been flogging a new gim-
mick called "hot rock cooking." According to the
pop-up folder they put on the night table in your room,
it's "the latest European restaurant trend—cooking
your own food on a hot rock at your table" (the one in
the restaurant downstairs, not the one by your bed).
Neither of us got to try this silly business on our last
pass through Calgary, but it occurred to us that this
"latest trend" is really nothing more than a pedestrian
version of engine cooking. The big difference is, when
you're done cooking on your hot rock you're still in
Calgary, while if you had fixed a nice veal cutlet on your
engine you'd be up in the mountains heading for Lake
Louise by the time it was done.

Still, for those of you who can't resist a new craze,
we have accommodated the hot-rock idea to car-engine
cookery. First, wedge the biggest rock you can up
against your exhaust manifold. Drive for about a week
to get it hot (depending on the direction you take, you
might still be in Alberta if you start out in Calgary). Now
stop your car, slap some food on the rock—unwrapped
—and wait for the edges to curl.

A word of warning: There's some odd food up in
the Canadian home of hot-rock cooking. At the same
Westin, the breakfast menu was hawking low-choles-
terol artificial eggs for omelets. When asked if the eggs
came from artificial chickens, the waitress replied, "No,
they're from Dome Petroleum."

TIMING, EQUIPMENT, AND SAFETY

When you set out to learn how to cook the way normal
people do, all you have to do is master the ways in which

different foods react to different treatments and temperatures—for example, the ability of egg whites to expand and hold air, the tendency of cream sauces containing egg to curdle if you get them too hot, and the fact that you can panfry a steak better in cast iron than in stainless steel painted with a token wash of copper. You don't have to go to the Cordon Bleu to learn these things, but if you do you can write a serious cookbook renouncing everything you were taught and yammering about how Western cuisine should be influenced by the dietary predilections of the !Kung people of Namibia.

You don't have to study under a despot in a *toque blanche* to learn car-engine cooking either, but it will help if you remember that you'll be dealing with the peculiarities not only of different foods, but of different engines. Nowhere does this come across more clearly than in the matter of timing. When we suggest times in our recipes, don't take us too seriously—and likewise, don't follow your own recipes chapter and verse when it comes to converting and timing them for use on the old V-6. *Experiment.* Something that took us four hours may take you two if you have access to a hotter part of the engine. Or the reverse may be true. About the only general rule we can lay down is that dishes almost always take longer to cook on a car engine than they do on a stove. Like we said, it's an inexact science. Relax and enjoy the scenery.

The down side to learning how to work a particular, beloved automobile engine like a six-burner Magic Chef is that you'll hate like hell to sell the car. The only consolation is that when you run the ad in the paper, you can throw in a come-on phrase such as "Cooks like a champ."

The equipment requirements for car-engine cooking are minimal. It helps to have an oven mitt or two, though there's nothing wrong with the old gloves you keep under the seat for shoveling snow and changing tires. It would be nice to mount a paper-towel dispenser under your dashboard, and maybe another for aluminum foil—it pays to keep extra foil on hand, so you can rewrap food after you tear the foil when checking to see if it's done. Beyond these basics, there exists the unexplored realm of specialty cooking equipment made only for use on car engines. We'd love to see a pot manufacturer come out with a line of covered vessels made to fit securely in the larger under-hood crevices of popular models—if for no other reason than the sheer pleasure of walking into a kitchen-gadget shop with a name like The Blue Nantucket Turnip and asking for a saucepan to fit an '86 Olds Cutlass Supreme. Or maybe auto-parts stores could sell them. Our other dream gadget is a lasagna pan that would slide into special flanges attached to the underside of the hood. (We can't figure out how this would work, though, without dumping tomato sauce onto the windshield wipers.)

A Kit for the Car Kitchen

If the scout motto "be prepared" remains a guiding principle in your life, you probably have stashed in your trunk a road emergency kit containing car-repair tools, a flashlight, spare fuses, flares, an ice scraper, and so forth. Why not be prepared for impromptu engine cooking as well? You never know when you'll pass a grocery store running a special on pork tenderloins.

In addition to an ample supply of aluminum foil and paper towels, here are some essential items with which the rolling kitchen ought to be equipped. Feel free to elaborate or simplify to the extent of your own ambition; what we've listed will see you through any of the recipes marked ▨▨▨ in Chapter Three.

—Eating utensils and plastic plates. If it won't make your car look ridiculous, carry one of those Edwardian baskets containing a Royal Doulton service for twelve.

—Small cutting board. Plastic is better than wood, since you probably won't be cleaning it right away. Wood retains bacteria if you don't scrub it pronto—that's why all those commercial butcher blocks wound up in trendy antique shops. Even if you do use plastic, wash it after every outing—especially if you've been cutting raw meat.

—A couple of sharp knives. A French chef's knife and a boning knife should cover all situations.

—Mixing bowl, two quarts at the most.

—Metal spoon for mixing. Wooden spoons are nice, but they present the same problem as the cutting board (see above).

—Plastic measuring cup.

—Pounding mallet. If you get one made out of rubber, you can also use it to knock out minor dents.

—Salt, pepper, and assorted spices: Pick out the ones you use most frequently. A plastic squeeze bottle full of cooking oil

> isn't a bad idea, but we wouldn't want to store it in a hot trunk too long.
> —Rubber gloves for handling the occasional hot pepper, when you can't wash your hands right away.
> —Can opener.
> —Oven mitt(s).

Remember, again, these critical safety tips: *Stay away from the accelerator linkage.* Don't move, remove, or block anything crucial to the car's operation. Always shut the engine off when you put food in to cook, and when you check to see if it's done. Avoid moving parts in general, especially pulleys, belts, and the radiator fan. (Get your fingers near that fan, and your car engine will become a food processor rather than a stove.)

PRACTICE RUNS: A COUPLE OF EASY FOOD CATEGORIES THAT WILL BREAK YOU IN AS A CAR-ENGINE COOK

For all our disparagement of the heat-a-can school of car-engine cookery, we nevertheless remember our roots at Schwartz's and also recognize that some timid souls will be looking for a way to ease into this wonderful new technology. Here, then, are a few tips on what we call the "ready-made" and "ready-bought" categories of food.

Around 1920, the Dadaist artist Marcel Duchamp shook up the world of aesthetics by attaching manufactured items such as snow shovels and porcelain urinals to gallery walls and calling the result art. Ready-made art, to be precise. Nowadays the giant food-processing companies, using supermarkets as their galleries, have taken a page out of Duchamp's book and offered us a vast array of ready-made food. It's manufactured, to be sure, and it can inspire the same sort of arguments as the stuff Duchamp put on display. Was that art? Is this food?

For better or worse, it's possible to pull off the highway into a supermarket lot anywhere in America and come out with something marginally resembling dinner —just heat on your engine and serve. The basic choices are to be found in either the canned-goods or frozen-foods sections. These suggestions are presented only for rank beginners and those in dire need of a car-cooked food fix; they involve about as much creative thought as trying to figure out whether to turn right into the Taco Bell or left into Long John Silver's.

Canned goods fall into two categories—liquid-packed, and semisolid mush. The first group includes such items as green beans, baby peas, Irish potatoes, and stewed tomatoes. The second takes in such crowd pleasers as corned-beef hash, baked beans, and dog food. For the automotive chef, the cooking methods are the same for either category. Punch a couple of small vent holes in the lid, cover lightly with a square of foil, and find a place—preferably on or close to the manifold —that allows as much direct contact with the can as possible. If simple wedging will not secure the can, perhaps shims of crumpled foil will help. (If you insist on being a classicist, try baling or picture-hanging wire.) The liquid-packed items will cook somewhat faster; if you overcook any of these, they'll just be even mushier than usual. If you overdo something like hash you'll get some crustiness around the edges, but this might actually improve the texture. At any rate, make sure the cans are securely in place and drive until steam comes out of the vents—maybe forty-five minutes to an hour for the average fifteen-ounce can.

Do not, **under *any* circumstances, try this procedure without punching the vent holes.** Without them, a can could explode under your hood. Even if it doesn't, you could still be in a lot of trouble. Just as the temperature of your antifreeze can rise above its boiling point because the system is sealed, an unvented cartridge of SpaghettiOs can get a lot hotter than 212 Fahrenheit. Remember the whooshing fountain you got last time you popped the cap on an overheated radiator before letting it cool? Imagine that fountain being full of superheated, sticky pasta, which will stick to you, and tin can shards, which will stick *into* you. We can give pretty close to a money-back guarantee this is what you'll get if you don't vent cans before heating. *Be warned!*

On the foolproof side, but showing no more imagination, are frozen foods. Just pick out your favorite, and shove it under the hood. Heating will take considerably less time if you defrost foods first, though this is best done in a refrigerator to prevent spoilage. Even at that, you may run into problems with sogginess when you predefrost. Not for nothing do the packages tell you, "Do not thaw before cooking." In any event, try to use some common sense: A small frozen loaf of garlic bread covers the business zone of most car engines a lot better than a twelve-inch frozen pizza. If you're using old-fashioned frozen food the aluminum packaging will already be in place; just wrap in an outer layer of foil and you're all set. If it's packaged for the microwave, rewrap it entirely in foil. Boiling bags are not recommended.

Obvious suggestions (virtually everything about frozen food is obvious) include shoving enchiladas or fish fillets between fuel-injection intake ports and jamming a Swiss-steak dinner on top of a manifold. Just remember that less-than-solid foods slip and slide. Try to cook a pizza vertically and you'll wind up with a dough disc rising majestically from a swamp of tomato puree and mozzarella. However, frozen peas loosely wrapped can be made to fit just about anywhere. Cooking times will range from about thirty minutes for loose vegetables to two hours or more for some of the beefier entrées.

If You Insist on Cooking Ready-mades...

As you may have gathered, we are not terribly enthusiastic about cooking off-the-shelf or "ready-made" foods on car engines. For one thing, they're too easy: How can you derive any sense of accomplishment from merely raising the temperature of something that's already been cooked in an industrial vat in Camden, New Jersey? For another, the realm of ready-mades has been getting shabbier and shabbier of late. Once there were just canned foods and frozen vegetables, but during the 1980s, the TV dinner crossbred with the microwave oven and strange new creatures were hatched. Supermarkets now devote entire freezers to bizarre vegetable-pasta—cheese sauce concoctions that can be either boiled in the bag or zapped in the micro, and "pocket" meals based on pita bread, croissants, and turnover dough. The vast majority of these things are designed to be microwaved while they're still frozen, and many are not suitable for the gentle heating a car engine offers even if you do take them out of their plastic bags, defrost partially or completely (see page 46), and foil-wrap them. But if you must cook the already cooked, there are a few standbys that always do well under the hood. Here are our choices:

—Hot dogs, knockwurst, kielbasa, and the whole family of precooked sausage products you'll find in the shrink-wrap section of your supermarket meat cooler. These have the advantage of cooking fast, and of being dispersible throughout the engine compartment should conditions so dictate. Best of all, they can be mixed and matched with two of the basic food groups,

—Sauerkraut and baked beans! In popular folklore, canned beans are usually depicted as the original car-cooked food. As we've mentioned, though, finding room for cans in today's engine-compartment environment is a chancy business (B&M's 7-ounce size opens up the most possibilities). The modern way to cook beans in transit is to empty a can into a foil packet, starting with a double thickness of foil to prevent tearing when you bring the sides up for wrapping. You can pop in a few frankfurters, whole or in chunks, and customize the package to fit just about anywhere—just be careful of sharp objects. The same goes for kraut. Either cook it separately, transferred from a plastic bag or can into foil, or make up a *choucroute garnie* that includes your favorite precooked wurst. Just drive until it's all heated through, usually an hour at most.

—Spam, and its cousins in the world of monosyllabic meat products. Spam has lost its allure for many of us who once loved it in the campfire days of childhood, but it does have the advantage of heating quickly, either whole (an engine Spam roast) or in individually wrapped slices tucked against engine hot-spots for that fried effect. Just plork it out of its can, and get the foil.

—Corned-beef hash. As malleable as baked beans but not as prone to leakage, hash is at its car-cooked best when you spread it into a flat foil package and do it up brown atop an injector housing that gets fairly hot. Foil-wedge for security, and turn once for uniform crisping. Now if only you could poach an egg somehow . . .

—Little canned hams. Back in the fifties, we thought these were the only things they made behind the iron curtain besides atom bombs. These Polish exports are still on the shelves, often in sizes small enough for engine cooking. As with Spam, all you have to do is de-can, foil-wrap either whole or in slices, and slip it onto the old mill.

Ready-boughts are a subject much closer to our hearts. The big difference between ready-mades and ready-boughts is individuality, and the intensity of the maker's intent. A good automotive analogy might be the difference between a so-called Indy Pace Car and a lowrider bopping down the bad end of Sunset Boulevard. Detroit pounds out a limited number of pace cars; the number is limited by how many saps will shell out several grand extra for the lettering on the side. (The first time we saw a "Pace Car" we almost believed it. Then we thought, What's it doing on Route 9 in Worcester, Massachusetts?)

A lowrider, on the other hand, is one of a kind. Someone makes it for himself, not particularly caring that BMW owners will chuckle at it condescendingly or that every third cop will pull him over if business is slow that day. One person decides how high the lifts will go, how purple the flocking will be. *He* decides how many dice will hang from the mirror, how many pictures of his mother will be painted on the doors. It's his car, and tough nuts to the rest of the world.

Food is the same way. Stouffer makes its stuffed chicken breasts according to a recipe calculated to offend the fewest number of potential eaters. Oregano? Too spicy for Minneapolis. Real provolone? Too ethnic for Memphis. Thyme? No, someone in Phoenix might realize it doesn't take that much time to do it yourself. It's like the Indy Pace Car: Make it seem distinctive, but keep it palatable to as many people as possible.

Now put those glaciated chicken breasts aside, and step into Tony's Delicatessen on 204th Street in the Bronx. (You can tell you're in the presence of an original, as Tony is an Italian running a traditionally Jewish business in a heavily Irish neighborhood.) Walk up to the display case and gaze at the potato logs. They're cylinders of mashed potatoes, rolled in bread crumbs and deep-fried, 50 cents each. Next to the logs, in keeping with the axle-and-wheel motif, are corned-beef *doughnuts!* These are made of finely ground corned beef, pressed into doughnut shapes, crumbed, and also deep-fried. Seventy-five cents apiece.

Why on earth would anyone make doughnuts out of corned beef? They're heavy as hell, and oily enough to require an EPA variance on the Arctic tundra. On the other hand, why not? Tony makes them and Tony likes them and that's good enough for Tony. Financially, it's a little better for Tony if you buy a few, but he doesn't really care. You're already in the deli, so you'll probably buy something. Who cares if it's a corned-beef doughnut or a meatball hero? Not Tony. Tony would like lowriders if he lived in East L.A.

Ready-boughts make for a marriage of two American ideals, freedom of choice and automobiles, and they are a natural for novice car-engine cooks. You could hop in your car and eat Tony's corned-beef doughnuts straight from the store, of course, but your hands would get so greasy that you'd lose control of your car on the Hutchinson River Parkway. The answer? Wrap 'em in foil, stick 'em on the manifold, and stop at the Mobil station near Mamaroneck to chow down. Just bring plenty of napkins.

A Few of Our Favorite Ready-boughts

Finding a great ready-bought is like driving east on Manhattan's Fifty-seventh Street on a late-June morning and watching the sun come up over the East River. (If this doesn't give you a sense of being present at the Creation, you may as well hire a chauffeur and ride around

slouched in the backseat with your eyes closed.)
Discovery is what life is all about, even if it's
only a greasy morsel to pop into your maw.

Here are a few of the morsels we've discovered:

—Corned-beef doughnuts. Even if you're
one of the many enemies of the mighty
Yankees, there's still a reason to visit the
Bronx. These leaden lunches are a sublime
melding of a form and a function that have
nothing to do with each other—yet in this
incarnation, corned beef and doughnuts
both make their leap at immortality.

—Piroshki. Bastardized spellings are always
a good clue that ready-boughts are nearby.
Stop in a little grocery on Russian Hill in
San Francisco and check the stock. Take
your pick of cheese, meat, or potato
wrapped in a huge hunk of dough the size
of a (ghaack!) McDonald's burger.

—Deviled crabs. The Hampton, Virginia,
restaurant was nothing more than two
house trailers stuck together, located
about a block from where the excursion
boats leave for tours of the Atlantic fleet's
mooring in Norfolk. Hampton may not
have a lot to offer besides easy parking and
cheap crabs, but what more do you need?
Pick up a couple, rewrap in foil (keep the
crabs in their little aluminum pans for form
and crispiness), and let 'em roast.

—Cornish pasties. These delicacies from
the Upper Peninsula of Michigan may be a

precursor of the idea of boil-in-the-bag meals, except you get to eat the bag. A hefty lunch of cubed meat, potatoes, and vegetables packed into a crescent (not a *croissant*) of stiff dough, it's perfect for munching while you're looking for grasshoppers in Nick Adams's dream fields along the Big Two-Hearted River.

—Coiled bologna. Gallon jars filled with a tight spiral of sausage look like a page out of Gray's Anatomy. They're handy because you can cut chunks customized to fit the nooks and crannies of your engine (not to be confused with the ignition coil).

—Stuffed peppers. Cruise the backwater towns of North Jersey until you find an Italian deli that stuffs its own peppers. You're looking for a bread stuffing heavy on the oil and garlic, something with the mean density of plutonium. The beauty of these is that you can drive from Paterson to Atlantic City with a couple of them on the engine and they won't get soggy. How could they? If they're made right, they already are soggy.

—Meatball on a half-pizza. Another Jersey delight. The "pizza" here is not the ubiquitous tomato pie, but a flat, round bread that splits neatly for stuffing—sort of like Middle Eastern pita, but thicker and breadier. If your meatball sandwich takes up a whole pizza bread, it's a "meatball wheel" (terminology courtesy Sterling's Delicatessen, West Side Avenue, Jersey City).

Ready-boughts are the forgotten flip side of the regional-cuisine trend, and places like Tony's and Schwartz's have their counterparts everywhere. In Kentucky, many small taverns serve rolled oysters—behemoth bivalves rolled and stuffed with cracker crumbs to the point of being a large bulge of cracker moistened with essence of oyster. In Rhode Island, the Shore Dinner Hall at the Rocky Point Amusement Park sells "clamcakes," balls of deep-fried dough studded with chunks of chopped clam. Going to Buffalo? Pass up the chicken wings and stop for some beef on weck, thinly sliced beef sandwiched into a sweetish caraway-seed roll. The list goes on and on: deviled crabs in Newport News, molded onto a thin piece of aluminum that will create a nice crusty bottom when it heats up. Gallon jars of coiled bologna, a North Carolina specialty—whenever you get peckish, just heat up about eight inches and keep driving. Cornish pasties, turnovers filled with meat and potatoes, are big in the iron-mining towns of Michigan's Upper Peninsula. All of these delightful ready-boughts are out there waiting to be wrapped in foil and savored on the road. There may never be a Northwest Passage, but there are still a lot of things in America worth discovering.

Car-Engine Recipes: Four American Regional Cuisines

America's new penchant for regional cuisines goes far beyond ready-boughts. Just when we thought the fast-food chains and the frozen-diet-dinner makers were about to do to our palates what broadcasting did to our ear for dialects, along came "American Regional." At its best, this trend has sparked a revival of the dishes your mother used to make—if her family lived in the same place for two hundred years. At its worst, it's inspired blackened cheeseburgers and a California cuisine that can be the gastronomic equivalent of New Age music.

Since we are loath to let the car-cooking concept miss this latest culinary bandwagon, we've chosen to arrange our favorite recipes geographically. We like to think that this way, they are true not only to the spirit and ingredients of the regions they represent, but also to the ambience of automobile travel in those places. What more perfect combination of experiences than to toodle along the rockbound coast of Maine with a cod poaching under your hood? (No, not a lobster. The little buggers crawl around and get caught in the fan belt.)

We've focused on four regions: the Northeast, the Midwest, the South, and California. If you think it cavalier of us to have left out the entire mountain time zone, just try to think of a characteristic cuisine associated with this vast, virtually unpopulated movie set. Salt Lake City? If you don't drink, don't eat. Denver? We covered oil under corned-beef doughnuts, on page 51.

A few words about cooking times: We've begun each recipe with a recommended mileage figure. Keeping in mind what we said earlier about time being a far more important factor than distance in car-engine cooking, we hasten to point out that our recipe mileage numbers are based upon an average speed of 55 MPH. Thus, a 110-mile recipe will take two hours to cook. (Just to keep things nice and clear, the time figure appears at the end of each recipe.) No, Mario, you *cannot* cut the cooking time in half by doubling your speed.

Finally, a note about storage before cooking. If you're leaving on a four-hour trip and you're planning to cook a two-hour dish, you'll want to keep your prewrapped food cool until it's time to put it on the engine. Unless it's wintertime and you're using your trunk as a fridge, bring a small cooler to keep perishables from spoiling in transit. If you have a really long haul ahead of you, you may even wish to freeze meals in advance, as we did on the rally. Attempt this only if you have a properly insulated cooler, and plenty of ice—and cook your meals immediately after thawing to prevent spoilage. We're not responsible for food poisoning due to improper refrigeration; consult a comprehensive cookbook or home-economics manual for the details of freezing and thawing.

> NOTE: **Recipes that can be put together on the road without any advance kitchen preparation are indicated by the symbol**

THE NORTHEAST

The Northeast, by our definition, takes in the New England and Middle Atlantic states. New England is where American cookery was born, and where it first acquired the simplicity, honesty, and hearty wholesomeness that have often, in the years since, degenerated into blandness. We have a theory that this downhill slide parallels

that of the native English stock, who originally must have been an interesting and adventuresome lot despite their wacky religion, but who have since been genetically transformed into such yawners that ethnics have taken control of the Massachusetts Republican party. But the best New England cuisine is still mighty satisfying, especially when it is based on the region's abundance of fresh seafood. This is a big plus for the car-engine cook, since fish cooks more quickly than anything on the old motor. Besides, if you can find enough room under your hood to heat up a can as well as a foil-wrapped fish, you can drive into Boston paying simultaneous tribute to the bean *and* the cod. Do it like the natives do, in a small, socially conscious car, and you'll be right in the Puritan swim.

The Middle Atlantic states, on the other hand, are so ethnic that the old-line ethnics aren't even considered ethnic anymore. They've run both political parties for years. This region's great contribution to American gastronomy has been Italian food, to which we pay homage in these pages. If you can cook it on an Italian car, congratulations—unless you still have a Fiat. A more realistic way to get into the spirit of Italian-American highway cookery is to tuck your foil-wrapped treats under the hood of a big white Caddy or a Lincoln Mark VII, pop Ol' Blue Eyes into the tape deck, and head out onto the Jersey Turnpike to do it Your Way.

NOTE: Because the Northeast has the most congested highways in the country, it is very important that you think in terms of time rather than distance when you are car-cooking up this way. Hit I-84 through Hartford at rush hour, and you could do a whole stuffed fish in the space of three exit ramps.

So, let's eat.

CUTLASS COD SUPREME

Cod, the "sacred fish" of New England, is the foundation of the region's vaunted white cuisine. (Note that in the second version of this recipe we have gotten risqué by adding two ingredients that actually have color—tarragon and paprika.)

Here's the basic version, which is a nice introductory recipe for car-cooking novices. It has all of three ingredients, and it's ready in a jiffy. What's more, it's ideal for impulsive eaters who like to be able to cruise up to the supermarket, breeze through the express lane, and put together their dinner right in the parking lot with no home prep work necessary.

Distance: 40–70 miles

4 cod fillets
4 tablespoons butter
1 tablespoon lemon juice

At home or on the road, using 1 or 2 tablespoons of the butter, grease 4 separate sheets of foil. Place a cod fillet on each sheet, dot with the remaining butter, and sprinkle with lemon juice. Wrap each fillet separately.

Cook 45 minutes to 1 hour and 15 minutes, depending on thickness of fillets and location on car engine.

If you want to get a little fancier and do some advance preparation in your kitchen, try this version.

To above ingredients, add:

2 tablespoons butter
1 small onion, very finely minced
1½ teaspoons dried tarragon
Paprika to taste

At home, melt butter and add onion, lemon juice, and tarragon. Arrange each fillet on a separate piece of foil, and brush both sides liberally with butter mixture. Dust with paprika and wrap.

Cook as on page 62.

HYUNDAI HALIBUT WITH FENNEL

New England fishermen used to call big halibut "doormats." For this recipe, get your steaks cut from one that looks more like a floor mat.

Distance: 55–85 miles

4 halibut steaks
1 teaspoon oregano
Grated rind of 2 lemons
1 clove garlic, minced
2 bulbs fresh fennel, thinly sliced
Dry vermouth or white wine

At home or on the road, lay halibut steaks on 4 pieces of buttered foil. Sprinkle each with oregano, lemon rind, and minced garlic. Add a generous layer of fennel slices and sprinkle with wine or vermouth. Wrap tightly.

Cook 1–1½ hours, depending on thickness and cooking location.

MERRITT PARKWAY VEAL SCALLOPINE

Winding its way through some of the most expensive residential real estate in the country, Connecticut's Merritt Parkway cries out for upscale recipes. This dish belongs on the engine of a Volvo, or maybe a Saab 9000 Turbo.

Distance: 35–40 miles

¾ pound veal scallops
½ teaspoon tarragon
4-ounce jar roasted peppers, drained
Salt and pepper to taste

At home or on the road, place slices of veal on counter (or on the board you carry in your trunk) and pound thin with the heel of your hand (or see **Abalone Allanté,** page 105). Give tarragon and peppers a whirl in the Cuisinart, or mince them finely with a knife. Place half of the veal scallops on individual pieces of buttered foil, spread with puree, season with salt and pepper, and top with the remaining scallops. Wrap.

Cook about 40 minutes.

If you want to get fancy you can roll the scallops with the puree jelly-roll style, one or two rolls to a package. Cooking time may be increased, but since the packages will be smaller you'll have more options as to where to put them. Be careful that they don't drop out into the road—the Merritt, like many scenic routes, is full of sharp curves, and if someone's Pirellis fail to get purchase on a red-pepper slick and they careen off into the trees, you'll be hearing from a very high-priced lawyer.

ENZO'S VEAL

In honor of the late Enzo Ferrari.

Distance: 75 miles

1 pound veal scallops
4 tablespoons minced sun-dried tomatoes
1 small red onion, finely minced
3 cloves garlic, minced
¼ pound prosciutto, sliced paper-thin
1 teaspoon dried rosemary, crushed
Salt and pepper to taste

At home or on the road, place slices of veal on counter (or on the board you carry in your trunk) and pound thin with the heel of your hand (or see **Abalone Allanté,** page 105). Arrange half of the scallops on individual pieces of buttered foil. Add a layer of sun-dried tomatoes, onion, and garlic. Cover with a couple of strips of prosciutto, and sprinkle with rosemary, salt, and pepper. Then top each with another veal scallop, and wrap tightly.

Start this in Manhattan and lunch will be ready in New Haven. Turn once, in Stamford. Total cooking time should be about 1 hour and 20 minutes.

EGGS-ON CHEESE PIE

This recipe, which originated in a medieval monastery, has also been adapted to the tuna-can school of injector-housing cookery. If cholesterol were measured in octane, this would be right up there with leaded super.

Distance: 55 miles

Bread crumbs
½ pound mozzarella, diced
6 eggs
Salt and pepper to taste

At home or on the road, butter the insides of six tuna cans. (Scale the recipe down if you don't have room for six cans on your engine.) Toss a couple of tablespoons of bread crumbs into each can, shake to distribute, and dump out the excess. Cover the bottom of the cans with about half of the diced mozzarella, then break an egg into each can. Add salt and pepper, then cover with the remaining mozzarella.

Cover tightly, as per **Eggs in Purgatory** (page 68), and make sure you have good contact with the engine surface. Cook about 1 hour, until cheese melts and eggs are set.

EGGS IN PURGATORY

You don't have to cook these in purgatory, but if you feel the penitential urge, make them while going around and around the Tonnelle Avenue traffic circle in Jersey City. The recipe works best on cars with a large horizontal cooking surface that gets fairly hot, such as the injector housing on a late-model Dodge Dynasty. It also involves the use of some auxiliary equipment, i.e., washed-out tuna or cat-food cans. These are handy items, by the way, to include in your road kitchen kit.

Distance: 55 miles

Spicy tomato sauce (either make your own or add a good amount of red-pepper flakes and/or hot sauce to a commercial variety)
Eggs

At home or on the road, butter the inside of the cans well, and into each one place about 5 tablespoons of tomato sauce. Break one egg into each can, being careful not to break the yolks, then cover with roughly another 5 tablespoons of sauce.

Tightly wrap each can in foil so there will be no spilling, and set them on your flat engine surface.

> **NOTE: make sure you do the foil-cone test for hood clearance, as outlined on page 24, before you try this recipe. If the cone smashes down to a height exactly the same as the cans, you're in luck—the insulation pad under the hood will hold them in place for you. If the space is smaller than the cans, give up. Think what a damned fool you'll look like with tuna-fish cans outlined in bas-relief on your hood. If the space is larger, use our foil wad security system (see page 24). But put the foil wads *under***

the cans, rather than over, because the cans will be soft on top.

If you can work out all these logistics, the cooking time on a hot engine should be about 1 hour. The idea is for the whites of the eggs to be set, with the yolks still runny. Uncover and poke whites gently to check.

PAT'S PROVOLONE PORSCHE POTATOES

As opposed to the couch variety.

Distance: 55 miles

½ pound new potatoes
1 cup milk
1 cup water
2 ounces aged provolone, grated
Butter

At home, peel potatoes and slice about ¼ inch thick. Place in saucepan with milk and water and simmer about 10 minutes. Drain and spread on heavily buttered foil—the number of packages you make is up to you, depending on the characteristics of your engine. We recommend at least 2, for optimum heat distribution. Sprinkle potatoes with the grated provolone and dot with butter. Then wrap.

Cook for about 1 hour.

SPEEDY SPEDINI

This is a classic Italian recipe. Stick these small bread-and-cheese sandwiches onto the mill in your Ferrari, and you'll be looking forward to stopping rather than speeding.

Distance: 40 miles

Small can (2 oz.) anchovy fillets
4 tablespoons chicken stock
1 small-diameter loaf of good-quality Italian bread, roughly 3 inches in diameter
³/4 pound mozzarella, preferably fresh

At home, drain anchovies and mash with a fork. Add chicken stock to make a thin paste. Slice bread into ½-inch rounds, and slice cheese into ¼-inch slices. Make triple-decker sandwiches, using 3 slices of bread and 2 slices of cheese for each, and brushing the inside surfaces of the bread with the anchovy spread. Wrap each sandwich individually in buttered foil.

Cook until cheese is runny, about 45 minutes.

THRUWAY THIGHS

This is a yupped-up version of that old New England tradition, poultry stuffed with oyster dressing. Cook it while driving to your condo in the "new Boston" or the "new Portland," or, if fate has so decreed, the new Lawrence, Massachusetts, which looks just like the old one.

Distance: 50–200 miles, depending on car (see below)

2 medium or 3 small leeks, white parts sliced thin
1 bulb of fennel, stalks sliced thin
4 tablespoons butter
½ cup chicken broth
1 dozen oysters, shucked, the liquor retained. (You can buy fresh or
  frozen oysters already shucked in the fish section of your
  supermarket.)
Salt and pepper to taste
8 chicken thighs, boned and butterflied

At home, gently sauté leeks and fennel in 2 tablespoons of the butter, then braise in chicken broth until soft. Drain, reserving the broth. Meanwhile, sauté the oysters in the remaining butter until their edges curl. Thoroughly combine leeks, fennel, and oysters (break up oysters, which will help you distribute them better), moistening with reserved chicken broth or oyster liquor if necessary. Add salt and pepper.

Now lay chicken thighs on individual pieces of buttered foil. Distribute the stuffing mixture among the thighs, folding one half of each thigh over the other and sealing tightly.

This delicious dish nicely illustrates the variations in cooking times among different engines. The first time we tried it, on a trip up the Maine coast in a 1988 Chrysler New Yorker (that was the same day we cooked the game hens on the injector housing), it took 3 hours and 45 minutes to cook

the thighs to perfection. Not that it wasn't worth the gas—
Alan Richman of *People* magazine, who was along for the ride
and the feed that day, granted us a "Hey, this stuff is really
good!" and gave the recipe its charming alliterative name.
But a couple of months later, in the hills near Santa Barbara,
an '88 Olds Cutlass did the job in only 50 minutes. The big
difference was that on the Chrysler, we placed the thighs in
and around the fuel-injector ports. On the Cutlass, they went
straight onto the exhaust manifold, which happened to be
very accessible. Good thing we didn't have the Chrysler out
there, because there wouldn't have been anyplace to stop for
fried clams while the chicken was cooking.

STUFFED WHOLE FISH

This is quite a production and is probably suited only to a large engine, maybe an old in-line six with a hefty side manifold. Use any firm-fleshed, nonoily fish. A small striped bass or large red snapper would be ideal. The presentation is much nicer with the head on, but you can take it off if space dictates. Headroom in cars isn't what it used to be.

Distance: Approximately 140 miles

1 stick butter
¾ pound fresh mushrooms, minced
1 pound fresh spinach
2 egg whites
Dash of nutmeg
Salt and pepper to taste
1 small red onion, finely minced
1 whole fish, about 3–4 pounds

At home, first prepare the stuffing. Melt the butter in a saucepan, and when foaming add the mushrooms. Stir and reduce heat to a simmer. Cook, stirring frequently, until liquid has evaporated and you're left with a creamy mass. Set aside. Rinse spinach and remove tough stems, then cook in a small amount of boiling water about 5–10 minutes. Drain, pressing out excess water, then chop very fine. Beat egg whites until frothy, and then blend with spinach, adding the nutmeg, salt, pepper, and onion.

Place the fish on a cutting board. With a thin boning knife, cut along both sides of the backbone from top to bottom of fish until the bone is free. Sever the backbone just behind the head and at the base of tail, and lift it out, leaving the two sides of fish joined at head and tail.

Carefully spread the spinach mixture between the fillets, topping with a layer of the mushroom mixture. Carefully wrap the fish in buttered foil, taking care to preserve its shape.

Cook about 2½ hours, turning once *(very carefully)*. If you can pull this off, we'll let you contribute to the next edition of *Manifold Destiny*.

SAFE-AT-ANY-SPEED STUFFED EGGPLANT

Italians aren't the only ethnics in the Middle Atlantic region. Like Ralph Nader, this dish has a Middle Eastern pedigree. Like the Corvair, if you handle it right you don't have to turn it over.

Distance: 165–220 miles

1 medium eggplant (approximately 1 pound)
¾ pound ground lamb
1 medium onion, chopped
1 clove garlic, minced
½ teaspoon ground coriander
Salt and pepper to taste

At home, split eggplant in half and scoop out inside, leaving ½ inch of flesh on hollowed shells. Dice the flesh you have scooped out, then set aside both the shells and the flesh. Lightly sauté lamb with onion, garlic, and seasonings. Toss with diced eggplant and sauté five minutes longer. Mound mixture in both halves of eggplant and wrap halves individually in foil.

Place on engine with skin side down. Plan a long trip; the cooking time will be 3–4 hours.

THE MIDWEST

The Midwest is where New England's solid Yankee fare took root on enormous prairie farms and in lunch-bucket industrial cities. Long hours spent in the fields or the foundry translate into prodigious appetites, which is how midwestern food got its reputation for density and heft. They don't serve "medallions" of anything out here, they serve manhole covers.

What's more, a funny thing happened to midwestern cookery on its way through the nineteenth century. It met up with the least subtle cuisine on earth, that of the Scandinavians and Central Europeans, who came to make machine tools and tend dairy cattle. If you think chicken and dumplings is serious business, how about a couple of pig's knuckles?

Finally, the midwestern palate has come to reflect midwesterners' status as the national control group. Why do you think the phrase "Will it play in Peoria"

came about? We'll give you a hint: It wasn't because Peoria is the home of the American avant-garde. It's the same with food. Midwestern cooking is common-denominator cooking. The folks there not only want plenty of it on the plate, they don't want it to be too weird. Our big food conglomerates know this, which is why they test-market new flavors of instant pudding in Iowa rather than lower Manhattan.

For the car-engine cook, the Midwest is hallowed ground. Not only is the native cuisine admirably suited to a cooking method that is imprecise, forgiving, and innocent of fine nuances, but it comes from the very same part of the country that gave us the American car in all its classic glory. Short of reciting the pledge of allegiance with a mouthful of apple pie, what could be more patriotic than cruising around the heartland with something nice and filling bubbling away on the engine block of a Detroit leviathan?

Last but not least, the Midwest is great driving country. No, not for harrowing downshifts on hairpin turns, but for cooking basic fare to the locally esteemed fare-thee-well while barreling down mind-numbing, four-hundred-mile straightaways. It's a perfect marriage of cuisine and terrain.

Just remember, in the Midwest *dinner* is what you cook in the morning and eat at noon. After an afternoon drive, it's *supper* you're taking off the engine.

MOM'S TUNA WIGGLE

Here's where we depart from the editorial "we" that has been making you think, erroneously, that we drive the same car, take the same trips, and eat the same food. "We" don't have the same Mom, either. Although Maynard's mother was born and raised in Rhode Island, her culinary spirit is pure heartland, and the following was a standard offering when he was a kid. It's food like this that makes people become cooks.

This is a quintessentially American dish that should be cooked on the engine of a quintessentially American car. We have in mind the revered Chevrolet Caprice Classic, which, along with the Caddy Brougham, is the last of the line of great rear-drive arks that once were the flagships of the General Motors fleet. "Caprice" is a funny name for this car, which is driven by the least capricious class of our citizens. No funny business here—just meat, potatoes, and a five-liter V-8. When the world has gotten so hip that there are only six Kiwanis members left, they'll hold their meeting in a Chevy Caprice. For this luncheon, we suggest Mom's Tuna Wiggle.

Distance: 55–1,000 miles

1 package frozen green peas
1 can light tuna in oil, drained and flaked

At home or on the road, thaw peas enough so that they can be separated. In a mixing bowl—or in a clean hubcap—combine peas with tuna. Dump the glop on a sheet of foil and make a reasonably neat package.

Throw it on the engine and cook for about 1 hour. The peas *should* be overdone.

NOTE: Since this makes a relatively soft package, it's ideal for molding around various odd shapes.

DWIGHT DAVID EISENHOWER
PEPPER STEAK

Note that we don't use the East Coast affectation *au poivre*. According to an old *Life* magazine, this was Ike's favorite food. It's a great recipe for cooking on the engine of some classic piece of 1950s Detroit iron.

Distance: Approximately 55 miles

4 tablespoons whole peppercorns
1 small strip steak, ½–¾ pound

At home or on the road, crush the peppercorns with a mallet, rolling pin, tire iron, or jack handle, then spread them over both sides of the steak, pressing them in with your fingers to make them stick. Wrap in foil.

Cook about ½ hour per side while driving through Kansas—longer, if not directly on an engine hot spot, or shorter if you like 'em rare.

HOT DOG SURPRISE

The surprise is that people still cook these. We first encountered them back in Cub Scout days, when Ike was still chowing down on pepper steak.

Distance: 40 miles

10 hot dogs
American cheese (or boutique-brand Wisconsin cheddar, if you have
an expensive car), sliced into hot dog—length fingers
10 slices bacon

At home or on the road, cut a deep slit in each wiener, and stuff with fingers of cheese. Then wrap on the diagonal, like an old bias-ply tire, with the bacon. Seal individually in foil.

These are great for stuffing into those odd places on the engine where you can't fit a turkey or a suckling pig. Cook about 45 minutes, or until cheese is melted and bacon is somewhat crisp.

JB'S MALL PUPS

This is great for those lazy Saturdays when all you feel like doing is cruising the malls. Since all the ingredients are already cooked, you can just leave them on the manifold and dip in for a few after a grueling stint in the Liz Claiborne sale section.

Distance: 25–30 miles

Two 5-ounce cans Vienna sausage
3 tablespoons cheap bourbon
1 teaspoon sugar

At home or on the road, neatly line up the sausages in a double row on a sheet of foil. Sprinkle with the bourbon and sugar. Seal neatly and add another layer of foil (we'll let you get away with just two layers on this one), pressing it tightly around the sausages so they'll brown.

They should be ready after half an hour on the engine, but are best eaten after the sugar caramelizes with the bourbon. Since car engines retain heat for quite a while after they're shut off, the sausages should stay warm for a long time—unless you run into a great sale.

MILWAUKEE TUBE STEAKS

No, not inner tubes. Drive west over the Milwaukee River heading away from the downtown financial district, turn left toward the Schlitz brewery, and you'll find yourself at Usinger's, home of some of the best commercially produced sausages in the United States. They run the gamut from fresh bratwurst, smoked bratwurst, and bauernwurst to things like blutwurst, which tastes like it's made from bad dreams.

Distance: 55–85 miles

Sausage—your choice
<u>Good</u> *mustard*

At home or on the road, smear butter on foil and put down a selection of fresh sausages, as many as you think your hottest engine-cooking spot will accommodate. Spread a little mustard over them and wrap. It's important to wrap the foil tightly around the sausages if you want them to brown, and not to leave any stranded in the center of the package.

Cook for 1–1½ hours, turning once, That should get you from Milwaukee to Sheboygan, where they have a distinctive style of bratwurst all their own.

OUT OF THE FIRE, ONTO THE ENGINE STEW

When we were lads, we both belonged to chapters of a uniformed organization devoted to woodcraft, knot-tying, and discipline. Looking back, we realize that the major purpose of this tent-raising and marching society was to keep boys occupied until they were old enough to drive. It's probably significant that the only conceivable activity they didn't award a badge for was driving.

We recently leafed through some of the recipes that got us through long, tedious, bug-bitten outings back in our paramilitary prepubescence, and came up with this number, ideally suited to motorized hiking. Put it on your block and see if anyone salutes.

Distance: 85 miles

¼ pound meat (any kind), cut in half-inch dice
3 vegetables you like (potatoes, carrots, onions, celeriac, etc.), cut in half-inch dice
Salt and pepper to taste

At home or on the road, mix ingredients and wrap in foil.

Originally we cooked this on the coals of a roaring campfire; since we're all grown-ups now, put it on the engine and drive for 1½ hours, turning at least once. (Don't blame us; it wasn't our idea to begin with.)

CANDY-APPLE RED CHICKEN

Why would anyone combine sugar with canned tomato sauce and Worcestershire sauce? Don't ask. A good midwestern guest eats what's put on his plate.

Distance: 85–110 miles

1 chicken breast, split
½ cup chopped onion
½ cup chopped green pepper
½ teaspoon garlic powder
1 teaspoon oregano
6-oz. can tomato sauce
4 teaspoons brown sugar
1 tablespoon Worcestershire sauce
4 tablespoons cider vinegar

At home, place each chicken breast half on a sheet of foil. Combine the remaining ingredients and ladle over the chicken. Wrap.

Cook 1½–2 hours.

CRUISE-CONTROL PORK TENDERLOIN

This is about as fancy as you dare get in the down-home Midwest, but it's OK if the pork tenderloin is from a native Iowa hog. The long cooking time will let you put a lot of prairie miles behind you. Just set the cruise control, line up your hood ornament with a distant landmark like the Nebraska State Capitol, and set a timer to wake you up when dinner is ready.

Distance: 250 miles

3 tablespoons Dijon mustard
2 tablespoons dry white wine
½ cup minced red onion
2 teaspoons dried rosemary, crushed
Salt and pepper to taste
1 pork tenderloin, 1–1½ pounds, butterflied

At home or on the road, blend mustard, wine, onion, and seasonings. Spread split surface of tenderloin with the mixture and press lightly together, then wrap with foil.

Find a medium-hot spot on the engine and turn once during cooking. Total cooking time should be about 4½ hours.

ANY-CITY CHICKEN WINGS

By now, "Buffalo" chicken wings have been consumed by millions who have no idea where Buffalo is, or that it is actually the threshold of the Great Midwest. This is perfectly fine, since most of the bar cooks who make them don't know where it is either. This recipe is based on the premise that since you can call something anything you want, you can also put anything you want into it.

Distance: 140–200 miles

18 chicken wings
1/2 cup tomato catsup
1 cup red wine vinegar
*4–6 canned jalapeño peppers, drained and minced (more if you like
    wings really hot)*
3 cloves garlic, minced
1 tablespoon oregano
1 teaspoon red-pepper flakes
Salt to taste

At home, place chicken wings in a bowl. Blend the remaining ingredients in a second bowl, and then pour over chicken wings. Cover tightly and refrigerate 24 hours, stirring occasionally. Drain wings, retaining marinade liquid, and divide them among 3 sheets of foil. Brush with remaining marinade.

Cook from Buffalo to Ashtabula, Ohio, if you know where either city is. Total cooking time will be about 2½ hours. If they aren't done at Ashtabula, press on to Cleveland (another hour down I-90).

LEAD FOOT STUFFED CABBAGE

Stuffed cabbage is a dish that can be pleasingly filling or heavy as lead, depending on what goes into it. In this version, the food sociologist can observe the effects of several generations of simplifying Americanization on an old East European favorite. Pop a few of these down your throat while you're pounding down some godforsaken stretch of rust-belt interstate, and the accumulated weight will sink all the way to your right foot.

> NOTE: **These are best prepared in a big Dodge with a YOU BETCHA DUPA I'M POLISH sticker on the rear bumper.**

Distance: 55 miles

1 small green cabbage
1 pound ground beef
1 cup uncooked rice
2 cubes beef bouillon
2 cans condensed tomato soup
Salt and pepper to taste

At home, separate the leaves of the cabbage, discarding the tough outer ones and removing the inner ones intact. Drop into boiling water. After 10 minutes, drain and rinse with cold water.

Cook beef in a skillet, breaking up with a spoon, until pink color is gone. Do not drain fat. Meanwhile, cook rice in two cups of water along with the bouillon cubes until water is absorbed and rice is done. Combine rice, meat, and 1 can soup (do not add water), and season with salt and pepper.

One by one, lay a blanched cabbage leaf flat, drop some stuffing on it, and roll up, forming a neat bundle with both ends sealed. Repeat until you run out of cabbage or stuffing.

Place the rolls on foil in pairs, smearing each with a generous amount of soup from the second can. Wrap.

Find a good place for them on the engine and drive about 1 hour, depending on the size of your cabbage leaves.

CURMUDGEON'S CAPERED LAMB

We'd like to end this section, which has been dedicated to traditional American values in food and cars, with a gratuitous gripe against bizarre additions to automobiles in the name of progress. One of the Japanese carmakers is coming out with dashboard-mounted display screens that show a map —of Tokyo, or, God forbid, some cloverleaf-happy midwestern city—with the best route to your punched-in destination lit up. This disturbs us on two counts. First, it is a direct refutation of the time-honored tradition of misleading or missing signage. As practiced in the approaches to Chicago, for instance, this gives a hapless driver the distinct impression that if he doesn't know where he is, he shouldn't be driving there. Given false confidence by the dashboard video maps, how many poor souls are going to be smashed into oblivion as they try to read a computer screen purporting to show the intersection of the Dan Ryan, Adlai Stevenson, and JFK expressways as they careen toward the Loop?

The other problem we have with this trend is that once it's been around for a few years, you'll be laughed off the road for being totally unhip if you don't have one of the damned things. (Why do you suppose there's an outfit in California making fake car phones?) The whole situation is not unlike the embarrassment you'd suffer in one of Manhattan's wear-all-black-and-make-sure-it's-too-big-for-you restaurants if you ordered lamb medium-well, and please hold the lingonberry and kimchi sauce. Women wouldn't look at you after that faux pas, even if you were wearing *two* Rolexes.

Lamb is like cars, and not only because they make a lot of both out in Middle America. Lamb gives you the opportunity to state your retro preferences, as in this midwestern recipe.

Distance: 55 miles

4 lamb chops
½ cup capers, drained and finely chopped
Juice of 1 lemon
Salt and pepper to taste

At home or on the road, sprinkle both sides of the chops with capers, lemon juice, salt, and pepper. Wrap snugly.

Cook about 1 hour, turning once. (This works best if you can get the chops flat against the exhaust manifold.) If you like them fashionably pink—if, say, you are driving east—cook for a shorter time.

TO GRANDMOTHER'S HOUSE ROAD TURKEY

Unless you haul the family around at holiday time in a Greyhound bus, you'd be pretty hard-pressed to engine-roast a whole turkey on the way to the in-laws. These individual portions will not only solve the space problem; when they're done, they'll keep the kids amused in the backseat. Afterward, cleaning up the mess can be made into a family game, with extra cookies for the one who finds the most shards of tinfoil in the upholstery. (Keep the used foil away from the dog if you want to have a happy holiday.)

Distance: 220 miles

1 boneless turkey breast, about 5 pounds, sliced into thin strips
  against the grain
3 large baking potatoes, peeled and diced
3 carrots, finely diced
Dry white wine
Flour for dredging
Salt and pepper to taste
¾ cup heavy cream

At home, combine the turkey, potatoes, and carrots in a bowl with wine to cover. Marinate for 2 hours in the refrigerator, then drain well (*don't* drink the wine). Setting the vegetables aside, dredge the turkey pieces in flour, then heavily butter 5 large squares of foil. Arrange equal amounts of turkey and vegetables on each square, and salt and pepper as desired. Cup foil around turkey and vegetables, and pour over each serving as much heavy cream as you can without making a soupy mess, then seal carefully.

Cook on the engine about 4 hours, turning once. We're assuming that Grandma doesn't live in the next town.

THE SOUTH

Practically overnight, it became fashionable to cook southern. Two distinct phenomena are responsible for America's sudden infatuation with Dixie at table. On the one hand, northern gastronomes finally realized that we have a native French cuisine within our borders after all, even if we did fail to capture Quebec during the Revolution. True, the culinary repertoire of Evangeline's Cajun descendants has crossbred with local influences that would make Montreal's eyes bug out, never mind Paris, but the result is a distinct cuisine that can be mighty tasty, even though done to death by local premix entrepreneurs and by gimmick-happy Yankee chefs who would blacken a doorstop if they thought somebody would buy it and eat it.

The other culinary trend that has turned America's attention southward is the craze for "comfort food." Lord knows all food should be comforting, but when

we started treating ourselves like finely tuned machines that run on oat bran and yogurt we somehow forgot that basic truth (we the society, not we the shameless omnivores who wrote this book). So now the pendulum swings back the other way, and we turn to the South for solace—i.e., calories.

The pickup truck is the obvious instrument of choice for cooking southern food, though a case could be made for a sedan with heavy-duty springs if you want to become a serious disciple of Paul Prudhomme. A Cajun comfort car, you might call it. As for the proper combination of culinary and driving styles, well, if you go screaming through some one-horse town late at night in a car with out-of-state plates, just be sure you're cooking something down-home. Imagine some beady-eyed Faulknerian cop asking you, "What's that smell, boy?" and then having to tell him that if he doesn't hurry up and write your ticket, the oysters in your Thruway Thighs are going to get overcooked.

Better you should be frying possum on that engine, boy.

GOOD AND SIMPLE
CAJUN SHRIMP/CRAYFISH

Driving down a highway like old U.S. 90, which goes east-west through Louisiana, you'll see lots of trucks in parking lots selling shrimp, crabs, and, if the season's right, crayfish. Stop and buy some, then go to the nearest vegetable stand and get some garlic, onions, and small green hot peppers. Now get cooking.

Distance: 35 miles

6 small green hot peppers
1 medium onion
2 cloves garlic
1 pound shrimp or crayfish tails, in their shells (if using shrimp, remove legs)

At home or on the road, remove seeds from peppers (a good reason to keep rubber gloves in your car), and mince finely, along with the onion and garlic. Spread shrimp or crayfish on heavily buttered foil and cover with the vegetables. Wrap.

Cook about 40 minutes, until shellfish are nice and pink. Cooking them in their shells adds flavor and gives you something to lick afterward.

"CAJUN" SHRIMP

On a recent trip through Louisiana we stopped to check out the shelves in a Pick and Pay supermarket in Lake Arthur. It was the first time we ever saw *gallon* jars of rendered pork fat in a butcher case. Next we browsed through the condiment and spice selections, and realized that a lot of what's been sweeping the country as "Cajun" cooking increasingly comes out of jars—jars of precooked roux, jars of spice mixes for meat and fish, jars with drawings of fat men on them. In short, what started out as a bona fide regional cuisine has become a premixed abomination designed to make fat people fatter. We don't know what the life expectancy is down there, but we do know that it's possible to travel through Cajun country for a week without encountering any food that isn't fried, with the exception of coffee and salad. Here's a sample, with the brand names deleted.

Distance: 55 miles

Rendered pork fat
1 pound shrimp from the supermarket
Assorted jars of whatever "Cajun" seasonings you've seen advertised

At home or on the road, heat fat until it liquefies. If you're a real diehard car cook, you might want to do this on an idling engine, using one of the cleaned-out tuna cans you keep on hand to make **Eggs in Purgatory** (page 68) in the Northeast. Peel shrimp and devein if they're large. Then dredge shrimp in fat and dust heavily with the powdered spices. Wrap in foil.

Place on a medium-hot part of the engine, and cook for about 1 hour. It doesn't matter if the shrimp are overcooked, since you're eating a concept, not a food.

BLACKENED ROADFISH

As in the previous recipe, think of the concept and not the food. What's important about this dish is driving along thinking, "I'm cooking blackened fish and you're not." It's the same idea as having a car that can go 150 MPH even if you never get it over 65.

Distance: 50 miles

1 pound firm white fish fillets, cut thin
Your choice of premixed "Cajun" spices

At home or on the road, cover fish on both sides with a heavy layer of spices, pressing them in with your hands. Place on foil spread with butter and wrap tightly.
  Cook about 25 minutes per side.

> **NOTE:** Some cars are decidedly better for this type of cooking than others. Take a cue from Cajun chefs, who heat their cast-iron skillets practically to the melting point, and go for an engine that has a maximum amount of exposed hot metal.

NEW ORLEANS DOVES

What to do after an afternoon of dove hunting? An evening of dove eating.

Distance: 40 miles

¼ cup butter
1 cup vinegar
1 teaspoon red-pepper flakes
1 tablespoon minced garlic
4 cleaned doves (two per person)

At home, melt butter and combine with vinegar, pepper, and garlic. Baste birds heavily, then wrap one or two to a package, depending on the space you have to accommodate them.

Cook about 45 minutes. (Start by placing birds on engine so that breasts are firmly against a hot surface, and turn halfway through cooking.)

U.S. 17 CAROLINA STUFFED CRABS

This solves the problem of live ones scurrying off the engine block.

Distance: 40–55 miles

6 large blue crabs
5 tablespoons butter
15 sprigs parsley, chopped
3 scallions, chopped
2 cups stale bread crumbs
Juice of 1 lemon

At home, boil crabs. Pick through meat and remove cartilage, reserving the shells. Melt 2 tablespoons butter in a saucepan and sauté parsley and scallions until limp. Add crabmeat and heat briefly. Then add bread crumbs, lemon juice, and enough cold water to make moist, firm stuffing. Fill crab shells, dot with additional butter, and wrap.

Bake in medium-hot engine crannies for 45 minutes to 1 hour.

PICKUP HAM STEAK

A lot of southern cooking, especially in the "comfort" category, seems to include staples like margarine and cheese. We're not saying it's good, but it's there. Enjoy it the way you might enjoy the decaying industrial landscape around Mobile or Memphis.

Distance: 85 miles

1 ham steak
Margarine
1 cup canned tomatoes, drained
¼ pound unsliced American cheese, grated
1 small onion, minced
1 bay leaf
2 tablespoons minced fresh parsley
Pepper to taste
¼ teaspoon thyme

At home, place ham steak on margarined foil. Combine all other ingredients, spread over ham, and seal tightly.

This can be a messy one. When you size up the cooking spots your engine affords, go for security rather than maximum heat. Don't worry about finding the manifold (the forty-five-degree slant of an '81 Toyota manifold has been known to cause a highway ham spill); this one is a natural for foil-wedging on top of the injector housing, or nestling in along the inside of a valve cover on an old V-8. Cook about 1½ hours; if it needs more time, leave the engine running while you stop in at a roadhouse for a Jim Beam and Coc'Cola.

CALIFORNIA

One morning while we were stuck in traffic on I-680 outside of San Jose, cursing the fact that our failure to get past the Bay Area before rush hour was going to cost us six hundred points in the One Lap of America rally, we noticed that we were idling next to a business-suited woman in a BMW 325 with a crystal hanging from her rear-view mirror. Not a graduation tassel, like in New Jersey, or a pair of fuzzy dice, like in East L.A., but a genuine crystal, possessed of God knows what secret powers—excluding, of course, the power to get a BMW out of Silicon Valley traffic jams. Right then and there it occurred to us that here was the very spirit of 1980s California, the perfect combination of mammon and mystery, the Bavarian and the Aquarian.

That be-crystaled Bimmer was emblematic of the California approach to food as well. The idea is to take expensive, high-quality ingredients, and combine them

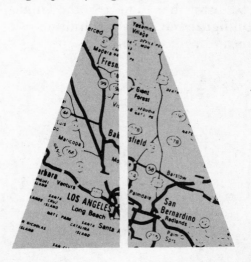

in such a way as to make people burble over how imaginative and creative you are. We're talking about things like venison steak with smoked kidney and fruit brandy, or swordfish smeared with pounded duck livers. (Honestly, we didn't make these up.) It also helps if there isn't enough to eat—if fasting raises your consciousness, maybe half-fasting will raise it at least partway. This half-fast concept could only have come from California.

Actually, we're not sure if what has become known as California Cuisine exists outside of the state's restaurants. Californians may not cook this way at home—but then again, they may not cook or eat at home at all. We know people in L.A. who are proud of the fact that they don't even own forks, let alone pots and pans; they just eat out all the time. But since they spend a good part of each day in their cars, engine cooking may be just what they need to get back in the habit of preparing meals for themselves, all the while saving money that would be better spent on real estate. To ease them back into cooking, we offer them a taste of the familiar. The rest of you can figure out how to substitute two pounds of sausage meat for the cilantro.

POACHED FISH PONTIAC

Pontiac is a many-splendored marque, several models of which fit in beautifully with the Southern California scene. For Malibu, we recommend a mint 1956 Safari wagon, preferably in white. For cruising Mulholland Drive at sunset, you can't go wrong with a 1967 GTO, in any color but that awful army-green they came out with. And over in the San Fernando Valley, it's got to be a late-model Trans-Am. Any one of them will cook this namesake fish dish to a turn.

Distance: 40 miles

One ¾-pound thick fillet of firm white fish native to Pacific waters,
    or a ¾-pound halibut steak
3–4 tablespoons dry vermouth or white wine
3 teaspoons minced shallots
1 bay leaf
Ground white pepper to taste
Butter

At home or on the road, lay out a sheet of foil and butter it lightly. Place the fish on the foil, then tuck up the sides of the foil and sprinkle the vermouth or wine over the fish. Spread the shallots on top, then add the bay leaf, pepper, and a few dabs of butter. Close foil carefully and wrap tightly.

    Cooking time is approximately 45 minutes; check after 30 minutes if fish is in direct contact with the manifold. The halibut steak will take longer than the fillet.

THREE-PEPPER SALMON STEAKS

This is the perfect recipe to fix while dashing down Route 1 along the California coast in your BMW. Keep an eye on your crystal; waves of energy will emanate from it when the salmon is done. If you want to be super trendy, place a foil package of romaine lettuce on your engine about 15 minutes before you and your crystal *think* the fish will be done. Next thing you know, you'll be serving salmon on wilted lettuce. To go with this dish, we recommend a nice bottled water, preferably a hard-to-find import.

Distance: 55 miles

1 tablespoon each black, pink, and green peppercorns, coarsely crushed (for the black and pink peppercorns, get out that tire iron)
Three 1-inch-thick salmon steaks (1 per person)
Olive oil (extra-virgin, natch)

At home or on the road, press the pepper into both sides of the salmon steaks. Brush with oil and wrap.

Cook about 1 hour, turning when halfway done.

ABALONE ALLANTÉ

Abalone is very hard to find, unless you are a member of one of California's protected colonies of sea otters. The only reason we're including a recipe here is so we can tell you how to tenderize it: Put the abalone flesh between clean pieces of ½-inch-thick plywood and drive back and forth over it a few times.

Distance: 25–30 miles

Fresh abalone, as much as your engine can accommodate
Lemon juice
Salt and pepper to taste

At home or on the road, place the tenderized pieces of abalone on well-buttered foil, and sprinkle with lemon juice, salt, and pepper. Wrap.

 Cook about 30 minutes on or near the exhaust manifold. While you drive, listen to Albinoni's Adagio on the tape deck. Now say "Abalone Allanté Albinoni's Adagio" five times fast.

BAKED GILROY GARLIC HIGHWAY 101

Gilroy, California, as the signs will tell you as you approach town on Route 101, is the garlic capital of America. This is a good dish to cook while on your way to a date that will probably fizzle anyway. The primary purpose of the bread crumbs, by the way, is to act as a reservoir of oil for the cooking process.

Distance: 55 miles

3 heads garlic (if you can find it, the so-called elephant garlic is spectacular for this dish)
¹/₂ cup coarse bread crumbs
California olive oil, preferably from a small grove that numbers its pressings and buys its bottle graphics from artists waiting to get their first wine-label contracts

At home, separate the cloves of garlic, but do not peel. Place the garlic and bread crumbs in separate bowls and cover with oil, soaking them for 1 hour. Drain, then package about 10 cloves to a serving, sprinkling well with the bread crumbs. (You can recycle oil for salad dressing.)

Place anywhere on the engine where there is a reasonable amount of heat, and cook until the garlic is very soft. You may be able to determine this without opening the packages. It should take about 1 hour.

MELROSE AVENUE CHICKEN

Here's a new dish from the heart of hip in Los Angeles. Eat this while wearing all-cotton clothing, in black, white, or nice bright colors, that is at least one size too big.

Distance: 55 miles

2 chicken breasts, boned and butterflied (1 breast per person)
Olive oil
1 green pepper
1 red pepper
2 yellow peppers (these cost the most, so it's important to use more of them)
¼ cup California olive oil (see preceding recipe)
Cilantro
Salt and white pepper to taste

At home, pound each breast with the heel of your hand until thin. Slice peppers thinly and sauté lightly in oil. Lay an assortment of peppers on each breast, add a few snips of cilantro, and season with salt and pepper. Flop each breast over in half to form a neat package, and wrap separately.

Cook on the engine for 1 hour, turning when halfway done.

CORVETTE STINGRAY

Skate, or ray, is a much-neglected food, probably because people have seen too many underwater horror films. A big advantage is that since it is neglected, it is usually cheap if you can find it. Since you will not find it frozen in a Kroger's in the Midwest, it passes muster as a trendy California food.

Distance: 55–85 miles

1 stick butter
1 small red onion, chopped
¼ cup capers, minced
1 skate wing, cut into serving pieces

At home, melt butter in a saucepan, add onions and capers, and simmer over very low heat about 15 minutes. Place pieces of skate on buttered foil, brush well with the onion-caper mixture, and wrap.

Cook 1–1½ hours on a medium-hot part of your engine, perhaps atop the injector housing. Be sure not to overcook, or you'll wind up with skate*board*, another California favorite.

CHICKEN BREAST LIDO

We named this dish after everyone's favorite auto corporation CEO, who recently began marketing his own line of olive oil from olives grown on his estate in Tuscany. If you can't find his brand, which is rated SAE 5W-30 for use in Chryslers, you can fall back on one of the better California oils.

Distance: Approximately 140 miles

2 ounces prosciutto, diced
1/2 cup shredded provolone
3 scallions, minced
1 chicken breast, boned and butterflied
Salt and pepper to taste
Olive oil

At home, mix together prosciutto, provolone, and scallions. Place half of the chicken breast smooth side down, then spread prosciutto mixture over it. Season with salt and pepper. Fold other half of breast over and press together gently. Place on foil that has been brushed with olive oil. Wrap.

Turn once during cooking. Cooking time, on a medium-hot spot, should be about 2½ hours, less if you have access to the manifold.

PARTING THOUGHTS

The world has seen only the beginning of car-engine cookery. A whole raft of questions waits to be answered: Should you cook a rump roast on a rear-engine car? How best to do brown rice on the wheezy little four-banger in back of a '67 VW bus? Is the Suzuki Samurai the ideal car for baking turnovers? Will someone who can afford a Range Rover please send us some game recipes? On a related topic, what's to be done about the tendency of English cars to cook everything twice as long as necessary? And finally, what exotic ethnic cuisines are about to emerge from under the hoods of New York City taxicabs?

If you have the answers to any of these questions, look for us on line at Schwartz's, on Boulevard St.-Laurent in Montreal.

Appendix

Recipe List by Region

	WHERE TO DO ADVANCE PREP WORK	APPROXIMATE DISTANCE/MILES
THE NORTHEAST		
Cutlass Cod Supreme (two versions)	Home/Road	40–70
Hyundai Halibut with Fennel	Home/Road	55–85
Merritt Parkway Veal Scallopine	Home/Road	35–40
Enzo's Veal	Home/Road	75
Eggs-on Cheese Pie	Home/Road	55
Eggs in Purgatory	Home/Road	55
Pat's Provolone Porsche Potatoes	Home	55
Speedy Spedini	Home	40
Thruway Thighs	Home	50–200

	WHERE TO DO ADVANCE PREP WORK	APPROXIMATE DISTANCE/MILES
Stuffed Whole Fish	Home	Approx. 140
Safe-at-Any-Speed Stuffed Eggplant	Home	165–220
THE MIDWEST		
Mom's Tuna Wiggle	Home/Road	55–1,000
Dwight David Eisenhower Pepper Steak	Home/Road	Approx. 55
Hot Dog Surprise	Home/Road	40
JB's Mall Pups	Home/Road	25–30
Milwaukee Tube Steaks	Home/Road	55–85
Out of the Fire, onto the Engine Stew	Home/Road	85
Candy-Apple Red Chicken	Home	85–110
Cruise-Control Pork Tenderloin	Home/Road	250
Any-City Chicken Wings	Home	140–200
Lead Foot Stuffed Cabbage	Home	55
Curmudgeon's Capered Lamb	Home/Road	55
To Grandmother's House Road Turkey	Home	220
THE SOUTH		
Good and Simple Cajun Shrimp/Crayfish	Home/Road	35
"Cajun" Shrimp	Home/Road	55
Blackened Roadfish	Home/Road	50
New Orleans Doves	Home	40
U.S. 17 Carolina Stuffed Crabs	Home	40–55
Pickup Ham Steak	Home	85

	WHERE TO DO ADVANCE PREP WORK	APPROXIMATE DISTANCE/MILES
CALIFORNIA		
Poached Fish Pontiac	Home/Road	40
Three-Pepper Salmon Steaks	Home/Road	55
Abalone Allanté	Home/Road	25–30
Baked Gilroy Garlic Highway 101	Home	55
Melrose Avenue Chicken	Home	55
Corvette Stingray	Home	55–85
Chicken Breast Lido	Home	Approx. 140

ABOUT THE AUTHORS

CHRIS MAYNARD is a professional photographer living in New York City. He is president and co-founder of the YO-YO School of Art.

BILL SCHELLER is the author of thirteen books, and serves as a contributing editor for *National Geographic Traveler*. He lives with his wife and young son in Massachusetts, where it is easy to find serious people and tie their shoelaces together.